Harriet Tubman

WOMEN OF FAITH SERIES

Amy Carmichael	*Harriet Tubman*
Catherine Marshall	*Isobel Kuhn*
Corrie ten Boom	*Joni*
Fanny Crosby	*Madame Guyon*
Florence Nightingale	*Mary Slessor*
Gladys Aylward	*Susanna Wesley*

MEN OF FAITH SERIES

Andrew Murray	*Jim Elliot*
Borden of Yale	*John Calvin*
Brother Andrew	*John Hyde*
C. S. Lewis	*John Newton*
Charles Colson	*John Paton*
Charles Finney	*John Wesley*
Charles Spurgeon	*Jonathan Goforth*
D. L. Moody	*Luis Palau*
David Brainerd	*Martin Luther*
E. M. Bounds	*Oswald Chambers*
Eric Liddell	*Samuel Morris*
George Muller	*William Booth*
Hudson Taylor	*William Carey*

WOMEN AND MEN OF FAITH

John and Betty Stam
Francis and Edith Schaeffer

OTHER BIOGRAPHIES FROM BETHANY HOUSE

Autobiography of Charles Finney
George MacDonald: Scotland's Beloved Storyteller
Hannah Whitall Smith
Janette Oke: A Heart for the Prairie
Miracle in the Mirror (Nita Edwards)
Of Whom the World Was Not Worthy (Jakob Kovac family)

Harriet Tubman

Rebecca Price Janney

BETHANY HOUSE PUBLISHERS
MINNEAPOLIS, MINNESOTA 55438

Harriet Tubman
Copyright © 1999
Rebecca Price Janney

Cover illustration by Joe Nordstrom

ISBN 0–7642–2182–5

Library of Congress Catalog Card Number 99–6542

Published by Bethany House Publishers
A Ministry of Bethany Fellowship International
11400 Hampshire Avenue South
Minneapolis, Minnesota 55438
www.bethanyhouse.com

Printed in the United States of America by
Bethany Press International,
Minneapolis, Minnesota 55438

REBECCA PRICE JANNEY is the author of thirteen books. A graduate of Lafayette College and Princeton Theological Seminary, she is a doctoral candidate at Biblical Theological Seminary. She and her husband live in Pennsylvania.

Contents

Introduction

Writing about Harriet Tubman has been a tremendous privilege, as well as a challenge; a privilege because she is one of the greatest women ever to have graced American history, a challenge because there is so little primary source information about her and the remarkable life she led.

She was an amazing woman, born into slavery, without rights, without any kind of privileges, without hope in any worldly sense. Nevertheless, Harriet Tubman fled slavery and later returned to the land of her bondage nineteen times to rescue some three hundred slaves. Things like that weren't supposed to happen, indeed never could have happened, had Harriet acted in her own strength. Instead, the woman who came to be known as "Moses" depended in an extraordinary way on the Lord Almighty.

In creating this book, I have been challenged to find the true details of Harriet's life. Because she was, like most slaves, illiterate, Harriet couldn't leave her own written legacy. Instead, she entrusted her story to biographer Sarah Hopkins Bradford.

Harriet Tubman: The Moses of Her People, first

published in 1869 as *Scenes in the Life of Harriet Tubman*, provided the foundational information of my own book. Nevertheless, there are often conflicting details about Harriet's life and times. Was she born in 1820 or 1821? At exactly what age did she work for the Cook family? Did she receive any compensation at all when she first went into the Union Army?

In order to provide answers to these and other questions, I consulted all the available sources. I also had an informative conversation with and correspondence from Harriet's great-niece, Mariline Wilkins. Then I speculated on the most probable solutions. Where there is a dispute about something, I have tried to present most sides of the argument, then put forth my own as well as my reasons for it. For the sake of ease of expression, and nothing else, I have decided to work with an 1820 birth date. Likewise, in the Bradford biography, long quotations by Harriet are presented exactly as the writer heard them expressed. "Dat" meant "that," "de" was "the," and "Linkum" was "Lincoln." Because such speech isn't familiar to today's readers, I have taken those exact quotes and substituted equivalent, contemporary words where necessary.

Some stories about Harriet's life have come down through the years with few details. We know little about her second husband, for example. Nor do we know exactly which of her brothers was Margaret Stewart's father or how he came to be free. In the account of a financial scam in which Harriet was deceived, biographer Earl Conrad didn't deal with how the swindlers specifically carried out their plan. In such cases, I attempted to "fill in the blanks" as best I could, basing my stories on educated guesses arising from other pertinent information. Regrettably, I am certain that somewhere along the way I have made mistakes.

After researching Harriet's life, I have concluded that she was remarkable for at least the following reasons:

- *Her close relationship with God.* She trusted Him completely—His love, His goodness, His mercy, His power to act on behalf of her deeply oppressed people.
- *Her lack of bitterness against those who persecuted her because of her race.* She accepted what couldn't be changed and changed what wasn't acceptable, all with malice toward none.
- *Her cheerful, optimistic spirit.* For someone who grew up in such squalid conditions, she focused not on what was, but dreamed things that never were and went forward.
- *Her iron-clad resolve to fulfill the unique mission God had given her.*
- *Her sacrificial giving.* Harriet Tubman poured out her life for others at great cost to herself.
- *Her way of bringing blacks and whites together.* She believed that for true advancement to take place among African-Americans there would have to be cooperation and goodwill between the races.
- *Her imperfections.* Harriet was magnificent, but she was, like everyone else, flawed. Sinful. Her story gives us hope that we can falter and still have an exciting relationship with God.

Harriet Tubman's life embodied the biblical principle " 'Not by might, nor by power, but by my Spirit,' says the Lord Almighty" (Zechariah 4:6). Everything in life seemed to be against Harriet. She was a victim if there ever was one, and yet she surrendered herself to God, who raised her up and used her in ways that paralleled the story of Moses.

In writing this book, I have been challenged to give my own life more fully, more trustingly, to God to use for His glory. May the same be true for you as you read it.

1

Harriet's Early Years

To many a slave yearning for freedom, Harriet Tubman was Moses, the deliverer. Some admirers spoke in awe of her being the tallest woman ever to have walked the earth, a person with eagle eyes and an acute sense of hearing. When hateful masters, who feared and despised her, sent their keenest, most vicious beasts in pursuit of her and her runaways, even those dogs cowered before her commanding presence. One of writer Frederick Douglass's biographers recorded dramatically that she roamed "through wilderness and over mountain . . . [a] hard-bitten creature with an animal's instinct for directions, with fang-like teeth and a horrible scar on her head, the result of a murderous blow dealt her in slavery by a crazed master. . . ."[1] *The Freeman's Record* of March 1865 summed up the effect of her life when it described her as "probably the most remarkable woman of this age."

When history's dust had settled around Harriet, the African-American author Pauline Hopkins put the

---

[1]Arna Bontemps, *Free at Last: The Life of Frederick Douglass* (New York: Dodd, Mead & Company, 1971), 211.

remarkable woman's life into some perspective:

> Harriet Tubman, though one of the earth's low-
> liest ones, displayed an amount of heroism in her
> character rarely possessed by those of any station
> in life. Her name deserves to be handed down to
> posterity side by side with those of Grace Darling,
> Joan of Arc, and Florence Nightingale; no one of
> them has shown more courage and power of en-
> durance in facing danger and death to relieve
> human suffering than this woman in her success-
> ful and heroic endeavors to reach and save all
> whom she might of her oppressed people.[2]

Harriet made her own escape from slavery in 1849
in order to make a better life in the North, not only for
herself, but for all oppressed blacks in the South. She
was determined to let God use her to rescue as many
of her people as possible. Indeed, in the years before
the Civil War, Harriet returned to that "Egypt" nineteen times, rescuing some three hundred slaves right
out from under the noses of their masters. No one else
made that number of trips or saved that many fugitives. That she lost not one of her "passengers" on the
Underground Railroad to freedom was no less than
miraculous. It is not surprising that she became the
most acclaimed figure of the secret network that ush-
ered slaves to the North, or that she became an almost
mythical figure in American history.

In truth, though, Harriet Tubman was not big or
invincible. She was among the most classic of under-
dogs. She never learned to read or write; she was female, a self-described ugly duckling, and a slave, of

---

[2]Sarah Bradford, *Harriet Tubman: The Moses of Her People* (first
published 1869; reprint, Secaucus, N. J.: The Citadel Press, 1961),
4.

little worth to anyone but her family. Her master only valued her for her ability to turn a profit. She was not much over five feet tall and suffered terribly from crippling headaches and sleeping spells because of a head wound she sustained in her youth. Harriet's voice was husky from untreated cases of childhood bronchitis and measles, contracted when she was forced to work in frigid water, looking after one master's muskrat traps. She also bore the cruel scars of countless whippings to the back of her neck. William Still, the Philadelphian who chronicled the stories of fugitive slaves, said, "Harriet was a woman of no pretensions, indeed a more ordinary specimen of humanity could hardly be found among the most unfortunate-looking farm hands of the south."[3]

Lacking money and education, her color, sex, and physical condition all working against her, Harriet had precious little to commend her to this world of beauty, wealth, power, and intellect. And yet having nothing she possessed everything. Her uniqueness lay partially in her courage, shrewdness, and complete devotion to her people's rescue, even at the cost of her own safety. Most of all, however, it lay in her unyielding commitment to, and faith in, her Lord Jesus Christ.

She was born Araminta Ross in 1820 on Maryland's eastern shore, and as she grew up started using her mother's name, Harriet. To the southwest of the small village of Cambridge was the Big Buckwater River, and near it, the Brodas plantation, where she and her family lived. Until the American Revolution, tobacco had been grown in the region; afterward, corn,

---

[3]William Still, *Underground Railroad Records* (Philadelphia: William Still, Publisher, 1883), 297.

wheat, and rye. Some of the farms, the Brodas plantation among them, became pastures for cows, sheep, and pigs. In addition to raising fowl and sheep, however, it also cultivated orchards of succulent peach, plum, apple, and pear trees.

About a hundred yards from the Brodases' "big house," Harriet grew up in a typical ramshackle slave shanty without windows and almost completely airless. "Its poor hungry boards rattled a raw kind of music when the wind blew."[4] Squeezed into that home with its hard-packed dirt floor, living mostly on salted fish or pork, cornmeal mush, and potatoes, were Harriet, her parents, Ben and Harriet Ross, and her five brothers and six sisters. She was the youngest of the children.

As a baby, Harriet was looked after by another slave whose job was to care for the children roughly five and under. This arrangement wasn't in order to give the youngsters a childhood—however brief—but because they were considered not yet mature enough physically to work in the fields or the big house.

Aside from the fact of her enslavement, Harriet enjoyed the beautiful Maryland countryside, as well as her closely knit family. Her youth abruptly ended, however, at about five, when she was sent to work in the fields of Edward Brodas. There she often pondered why a slave's life should be so hard and dreamed of someday being free.

At the age of thirteen, Harriet had her first experience in helping a slave escape. One evening in the late fall she was working in the fields of a man named Barrett when she saw Jim, one of his slaves, slip away

---

[4]Earl Conrad, *Harriet Tubman* (Washington, D.C.: The Associated Publishers, Inc., 1943), 3.

to the village store without permission. Harriet watched in dread as the overseer followed Jim. She quickly decided to make a dash through the fields ahead of the supervisor so she could warn the slave. It was too late, however.

In the store a tense confrontation ensued. The overseer commanded the sturdily built Harriet to help restrain Jim so he could be whipped. Harriet refused, then bravely blocked the door with her own body so that Jim could make a getaway. The enraged overseer yanked a two-pound lead weight from the store's scales and hurled it in Jim's direction. He missed his target, though, and the weight struck Harriet's forehead. She crumpled to the floor as though dead. The impact fractured her skull and created a great convex dent.

For two months Harriet lay in a corner of the Ross cabin on a bundle of rags, delirious, not recognizing anyone. Her mother lovingly nursed the young woman, praying her back to life and health when almost everyone else had given up on Harriet, including Edward Brodas. When he determined that she wouldn't be good anymore in the fields, Brodas tried to sell Harriet. No one, however, who came to look at her would have anything to do with such damaged goods. She seemed much too far gone to be of any use to them.

As Harriet's physical strength slowly improved, her spiritual maturity and resolve against slavery deepened. In the long run, wrote Sarah Bradford, the incident with the lead weight "is the key to the later Harriet Tubman: for if a woman's life ever contained a youthful episode which was a lever to unlock all of the other facets of her being, that incident was such a one."[5] Harriet's great-niece, Mariline Wilkins, believed it was a powerful impetus for Harriet's desire to help end slavery. "When she was struck with the two-pound weight," Wilkins commented, "she prayed to her God to help her get rid of this awful institution of slavery." Indeed, the accident deepened Harriet's faith. She began to pray "without ceasing" about the direction of her own life.

That Christmas, Harriet also began a months-long conversation with God about her master. In it she prayed fervently for Brodas' conversion, asking the Lord either to change his heart or let him die.

> [I would pray] "Oh, dear Lord, change that man's heart, and make him a Christian." And all the time he was bringing men to look at me, and they stood there saying what they would give, and what they would take, and all I could say was, "Oh, Lord, convert old master."[6]

While recuperating, Harriet faced a new calamity. Rumors reached her that as soon as she was able to move, she and her brothers were going to be sold to a chain gang far into the South. There, planters would buy them at an auction as if they were horses or sheep. Harriet couldn't imagine anything worse, not even death. She adored her family and couldn't bear the prospect of never seeing them again in this life. She also had heard of the South's brutally hot weather and large cotton and tobacco plantations where she probably would become an insignificant cog.

At this point, she altered the tone of her prayers for Brodas.

---

[5]Bradford, 25.
[6]Ibid., 24.

I changed my prayer, and I said, "Lord, if you ain't never going to change that man's heart, kill him, Lord, and take him out of the way, so he won't do no more mischief." Next things I heard old master was dead; and he died just as he had lived, a wicked, bad man.[7]

The death of Brodas greatly troubled Harriet. Her prayers had been his ruination, she thought, and she would give anything to get "that poor soul" back. Finally, though, Harriet resigned herself to his death being God's will, not just her own.

Judged unfit to work in the fields, Harriet was hired out by her new master's guardian, Dr. Thompson, to James and Susan Cook, weavers who lived about ten miles away. (Brodas' heir was too young to take over operations of the plantation.) The Cooks had just had a baby and needed someone to look after the child.

"Miss Susan" expected no nonsense from Harriet, who quickly discovered that her job description wasn't limited to the overall care and feeding of the baby. Instead, Harriet was expected to do anything and everything that Miss Susan wanted. On the first morning of Harriet's sojourn there, Miss Susan gave her a thorough whipping about the face and neck four times— before breakfast. In fact, Susan Cook began each day with a lashing, using a rawhide switch that she kept on a shelf above her bed. The beatings were a horror to the slave girl, who quickly learned to protect herself as much as possible by putting on all the thick clothes she had. Harriet also discovered that if she put on a really convincing act, screaming in pain when the whip came down, Miss Susan would be satisfied that

---

[7]Conrad, 14.

the thrashing had been effective and would stop sooner.

Unfortunately, the whip wasn't just reserved for the first thing in the morning. Every little thing Harriet did that displeased Miss Susan was cause to inflict the instrument of torture. When she told the girl to dust the house, for example, Harriet did her best, but no one had ever shown her how to dust. She had worked in the fields, not in the big house. Miss Susan verbally and physically lashed out at Harriet for her "stupidity," then sent her back to re-dust the parlor. This scene repeated five times. Miss Susan was so brutal with her tongue, as well as the whip, that her sister, who was staying in the house at the time, was awakened by the noise and went to investigate. After sizing up the situation, she asked, "Why do you whip the child, Susan, for not doing what she has never been taught to do? Leave her to me a few minutes, and you will see that she will soon learn how to sweep and dust a room."[8] The problem was quickly rectified.

The Cooks inflicted other kinds of mistreatment upon Harriet. They never gave her enough to eat, for one thing. In addition, they required her to spend long nights watching their baby. If the child cried even once, it meant that Harriet was neglecting her duties. She was whipped every time the baby fussed. One Friday morning Miss Susan was holding the child after breakfast as she and her husband engaged in a stormy argument. As Harriet stood by waiting to take over, her stomach growling, she noticed a bowl on the kitchen table containing lumps of white sugar. Recalling the episode in later years, she said:

That sugar, right by me, did look so nice . . . so

---

[8]Bradford, 19.

I just put my fingers in the sugar bowl to take one lump and maybe she heard me for she turned and saw me. The next minute she had the rawhide down. I gave one jump out of the door and I saw that they came after me, but I just flew and they didn't catch me. I ran and I ran and I passed many a house, but I didn't dare to stop for they all knew my mistress and they would send me back.[9]

Harriet, starved and shaking with fear, took refuge in a pigpen for five days. "The old sow would push me away when I tried to get her children's food, and I was awfully afraid of her."[10] By that Tuesday, Harriet was so famished that she decided to return to the heartless Miss Susan because at least she would get something, no matter how inadequate, to fill her empty stomach. She knew full well, however, that her return would also be grounds for another beating. "I didn't have anywhere to go, even though I knew what was coming," Harriet said. "So I went back."[11]

Despite their whippings, unreasonable orders, and inadequate provisions, the Cooks gave Harriet the opportunity to participate in their family prayers. She always flatly refused, though, because her sensitive and discerning spirit could see right through their hypocrisy. Instead of praying with them, she would go off at a distance and ask God to make her strong and able to fight the brutality of slavery.

Because the Cooks thought Harriet did so poorly with domestic chores, Mr. Cook ended up using her to watch his muskrat traps outside. It mattered not at all to him that she caught a severe case of the measles

---

[9]Conrad, 9.
[10]Ibid.
[11]Ibid., 10.

while wading in the cold water. Wade she must, until Harriet finally dropped from illness, exposure, malnutrition, and exhaustion. At that point the Cooks sent her back in disgust to the Brodas plantation saying that she wasn't "worth a sixpence."[12] It fell to Harriet's mother, "Old Rit," to nurse her back to health once again, spreading lard over Harriet's scarred neck and soothing her bent, though not broken, spirit.

Harriet said that when she looked back on her difficult childhood circumstances, she didn't blame those who had inflicted pain upon her for their cruelty. She believed that they simply hadn't known any better. She blamed it on the way they were brought up, "with the whip in their hands." She would add that it "wasn't the way on all plantations; there were good masters and mistresses, as I've heard tell, but I didn't happen to come across any of them."[13]

When Harriet was well enough to work, she was hired out once again as a nurse and housekeeper. Unfortunately, her new mistress proved to be as mean-spirited as Miss Susan and whipped Harriet five or six times a day. After extracting every last ounce of Harriet's strength, the woman sent her back to the Brodas homestead, where Old Rit again nursed her daughter's injuries.

At last, Harriet returned to work as a field hand, enjoying it far more than being inside taking care of someone's house or children. She enjoyed the outdoors, where she also got to work near her father. He would teach her and her brothers songs as they labored, as well as how to read signs of the weather and ocean tides. He also told them how to understand and

[12]Bradford, 21.
[13]Conrad, 10.

get along in the woods. At night, when the work was done, the slaves would often sing along to banjo music, and then the older ones would tell vivid stories about their earlier lives in Africa. Harriet learned that her own grandparents on both sides had endured the Middle Passage sometime between 1725 and 1750 and that they were from the Ashanti kingdom of western Africa. There the people had resisted British invasions for four centuries. (They succumbed to colonization in 1896.) Harriet was a tenderhearted young woman who sometimes cried herself to sleep when she thought about what had befallen so many of her people.

Harriet became very strong physically and more alert mentally even though the attack with the lead weight had left her with a lifelong handicap. A strange sleeping sickness caused her to fall asleep suddenly at any time and any place and without warning. The malady followed a somewhat predictable pattern, though. If Harriet was still for more than fifteen minutes, she would fall asleep. Sometimes her mouth went slack and her eyes glazed over, giving her the appearance of one who was half-witted. The slumber was not refreshing, either; she would awaken exhausted with a feeling of heaviness. She once said that she liked to keep busy with physical activity and enjoyed being in the sun, probably because such conditions enabled her to stay alert. In fact, she became so robust that John Stewart, a master for whom she worked in the timber business, regarded her as something of a showpiece. He often summoned the young woman before his friends to give exhibitions of her physical prowess. She could cut half a cord of wood a day—more than most men—but she never liked to be the center of that kind of attention.

Harriet endured many hardships in her tumultuous youth and early adulthood, but it was all about to work out for a good purpose. As her biographer Sarah Bradford said, "God had a great work for her to do in the world, and the discipline and hardship through which she passed in her early years were only preparing her for her [later] life of adventure and trial."[14]

---

[14]Bradford, 16.

2

A Deep Faith

The key to understanding Harriet Tubman and her role in overturning American slavery is her faith in Jesus Christ. That relationship originated in the earliest days of her childhood and became intertwined with a passionate desire and a special calling to relieve in some way her people's oppression. Harriet never considered undertaking such a formidable crusade in her own strength. She knew in her heart that apart from the Lord working within her—poor, female, and illiterate as she was—she could do nothing.

There didn't seem to be a time when Harriet did not trust the Lord completely with her life. Nor was the extent of her praying limited to once in the morning and again at night. Rather, she had an ongoing conversation with God, which resulted in an intimate association with Him.

Harriet's unyielding faith began with her parents, who had their own earnest relationships with the Lord. Indeed, for these humanly forsaken people, without worldly goods or security of any kind, faith was their richest legacy, something no law or slave owner could prevent them from passing on to their children. Their bodies might not have been their own, but their spirits were. Harriet's parents, Harriet and Ben Ross, came to believe that if white people would practice what they said they believed about the Lord Jesus, life for blacks would be different. (It isn't clear whether this implied whites would treat their slaves better or emancipate them altogether.)

Even as a little girl, Harriet longed to be free. She constantly dreamed of her people's liberation. Her parents got nervous whenever they heard her talking about it, though, warning her that it was dangerous to mention such things, let alone try to run away. What chance did a fugitive slave have when the masters networked among themselves, on the lookout for slaves gone AWOL, employing powerful hunting dogs and invoking the law in their searches? Instead, Ben Ross encouraged his firebrand of a daughter to trust her future entirely to the good Lord. Ben was a stable and strong man whose religious faith gave him an irrepressible sense of hope about life, something he instilled in his youngest daughter. He simply told Harriet, "Child, don't fret so about it all. Heed God and be as good as you best know how to be."[1]

After nearly being killed by the lead weight, Harriet's prayers for her master were evidence of how the Lord was protecting her spirit from a potentially debilitating bitterness toward the people and forces that kept her down. They also revealed a strong sense of discernment. Although Edward Brodas was no doubt considered an upstanding Christian man by his white neighbors in Dorchester County, Harriet couldn't believe that a true follower of Christ would behave as

---

[1]Conrad, 11.

her master did. She was particularly upset with him when he sold two of her sisters to Deep South slave-holders, causing intense heartache within her family. That she prayed for Brodas' conversion also indicates a concern for his eternal soul as well as her belief that if he did come to faith in Christ, Brodas would be a changed man toward his slaves.

Harriet also kept up a kind of running conversation with the Lord about the state of her own soul. She told Sarah Bradford:

> I prayed all the time, about my work, everywhere; I was always talking to the Lord. When I went to the horse trough to wash my face, and took up the water in my hands, I said, "Oh, Lord, wash me, make me clean." When I took up the towel to wipe my face and hands, I cried, "Oh, Lord, for Jesus' sake, wipe away all my sins!" When I took up the broom and began to sweep, I groaned, "Oh, Lord, whatsoever sin there be in my heart, sweep it out, Lord, clear and clean."[2]

Along with her candid and fervent requests of God, Harriet spent her time learning and committing Bible passages to memory, ones that would provide great encouragement throughout her life. Not surprisingly, one of her favorites was Isaiah 16:3, a verse that reveals what was in her heart about her future as a free woman: "Hide the fugitives, do not betray the refugees." Some twenty years before she became Moses to her people, leading them from Egypt, God was preparing her, body and soul, for her great work. Not even the ill effects of a vile head wound could thwart that plan.

---

[2]Bradford, 25.

Throughout her life, Harriet maintained a child-like dependence on the Lord to sustain her and those for whom He had given her responsibility. Her relationship with God was intimate and acute, almost tactile. Mariline Wilkins said of her great-aunt, "Harriet Tubman never put anything ahead of God. She never did anything without discussing it with her God, and she always got her answers." In an article published during Harriet's lifetime, the writer commented,

> Her whole soul was filled with awe of the mysterious Unseen Presence, which thrilled her with such depths of emotion that all other care and fear vanished. Then she seemed to speak with her Maker "as a man talketh with his friend;" her childlike petitions had direct answers, and beautiful visions lifted her up above all doubt and anxiety into serene trust and faith. No man can be a hero without this faith in some form; the sense that he walks not in his own strength, but leaning on an almighty arm. Call it fate, destiny, what you will; Moses of old, Moses of today, believed it to be Almighty God.[3]

Harriet's intense faith also had as a component a prophetic ability that would prove critical to her work rescuing slaves. Sometimes she would be warned by visionlike dreams or omens of impending trouble. Other times, she was given a joyful glimpse of wonderful things to come. One particularly vivid and recurring dream originated in her youth. In it she could see a line that divided slavery from freedom, which was, of course, the Mason and Dixon border, except that at a young age she didn't know anything about it.

[3]Charles L. Blockson, *The Underground Railroad in Pennsylvania* (Jacksonville, N.C.: Flame International, 1981), 122.

On the northern side people stood reaching out their hands across the line, calling her by the name of Moses and asking her to come across.

As an adult, Harriet said that before she escaped from Maryland she often had dreams in which she flew like a bird over fields, mountains, towns, and water before running out of strength. Then, as she started to descend, a woman dressed in white would come to her rescue. When in 1849 Harriet actually did escape to the North, all along the way she was amazed when she recognized places she traveled through because she had dreamed of them so many times. Several women who assisted her in her flight had also made earlier appearances in those dreams.

When Harriet told people about her unusual yet wonderful experiences, they sometimes had difficulty believing her. In her book about the slave liberator, Sarah Bradford admitted that at times even she found Harriet's stories about the supernatural ways God dealt with her to border on the fantastic. Had she not known Harriet and her rock solid character, Bradford said that she could not have believed her.[4]

Bradford was so concerned that Harriet's stories might be met with skepticism or derision that she included in her book several letters from prominent nineteenth-century people who vouched for Harriet's complete spiritual integrity. That included orator Frederick Douglass, statesman William H. Seward, and abolitionist Wendell Phillips. In addition, Congressman Gerrit Smith, whose efforts helped lead to the founding of the anti-slave Republican Party, told Bradford, "I have often listened to Harriet with delight on her visits to my family, and I am convinced

---

[4]Bradford, 75–76.

that she is not only truthful, but that she has a rare discernment. . . ."[5]

Sarah Bradford went a step further to assure her readers that Harriet was genuine about her supernatural experiences. Bradford admitted that when she wrote the first edition of her book about Harriet, she had done so under severe time constraints. Lest anyone find fault with her accounts of Harriet's close relationship with the Lord, however, Bradford said, "So far as it has been possible, I have received corroboration of every incident related to me by my heroic friend."[6] While she had heard other amazing stories about God's work in Harriet's life, Bradford refused to use any that she could not verify personally. She concluded, "No one can hear Harriet talk and not believe every word she says. As Mr. Sanborn [Franklin Sanborn, a prominent journalist] says of her, 'she is too real a person not to be true.' "[7]

Harriet told Bradford many touching incidents of how the Lord had worked in her life, including a memorable one that happened in 1860, three years before the Emancipation Proclamation. At the time, Harriet was staying in New York at the home of a black pastor, the Reverend Henry Highland Garnet. One night she had what seems to have been a prophetic dream. When she woke up, she went to her friends at breakfast, beaming all over. When they asked her what had happened to her, Harriet called out in a loud and exuberant voice, "My people are free! My people are free!" She was so excited that she couldn't eat a bite. Garnet became upset with her. "Oh, Harriet! Harriet!" he said. "You've come to torment us before the time;

---

[5]Ibid., 76.
[6]Ibid., 5.
[7]Ibid.

do cease this noise!" Then he added soberly, "My grandchildren may see the day of emancipation of our people, but you and I will never see it." That did not dampen Harriet's ardor in the least. "I tell you, sir," she said, "you'll see it, and you'll see it soon. My people are free!"[8]

When Abraham Lincoln issued his Emancipation Proclamation in 1863, Harriet's friends had a difficult time understanding why she wasn't excited. Hadn't all that she had been working so hard for finally come to pass? In a reference to that earlier dream at Pastor Garnet's house, she told them, "Oh, I had my jubilee three years ago. I rejoiced all I could then. I can't rejoice no more."[9]

The way the Lord spoke to Harriet wasn't just mysterious; it was also practical in how it helped her rescue slaves. In particular, Harriet had a powerful sense of discernment. She could tell whether people were for her or against her. Harriet also "knew" when danger was present because she had strong premonitions that manifested themselves physically. She described to the Boston Commonwealth in 1863 that her heart would flutter oddly whenever she felt threatened. At such a time, she said, "They may say 'peace, peace' as much as they like, but I know it's going to be war!"[10] According to Harriet, her father also had a similar gift; for example, she said that he had foreseen the coming of the Mexican War of 1846 to 1848.[11]

Harriet's faith was not, of course, all signs and wonders, and she didn't think she was remarkable because God spoke to her above the realm of the normal.

---

[8]Ibid., 92–93.
[9]Ibid.
[10]Ibid., 115.
[11]Ibid.

At the heart of it was a rock solid trust in the all-powerful Creator, who cared intimately for her and the rest of her people. She didn't expect to be coddled by Him, either, because of her spiritual gifts, or to have Him make her way in life comfortable or painless. She certainly didn't take any credit for her successes in rescuing slaves. That, she insisted, belonged only to God. She was merely His vessel to bring comfort to her persecuted people.

Oliver Johnson, an abolitionist, told a story of the time Harriet came to visit him in New York City while an anti-slavery woman from Boston also was there. Harriet began to tell them about her latest rescue and how she spent one night waiting in the woods for a party of slaves to rendezvous with her. They never came. She spent that dreary night in a severe snowstorm that raged around her, trying to gain some semblance of warmth and protection by huddling at the base of a tree. The white woman who was listening to the story became deeply upset about what had happened that night. "Why, Harriet," she said. "Didn't you almost feel when you were lying alone as if there was no God?" Harriet didn't see it that way at all, though, and her straightforward response set the woman straight. "Oh, no, missus! I just asked Jesus to take care of me, and He never let me get frostbitten one bit."[12]

Harriet's admirers couldn't get over how, in the face of terrible danger, with the odds against her, she had such a vital sense of hope, joy, and fearlessness. How could she march straight into the enemy camp and attempt the most incredible rescues anyone could imagine? The reason, she insisted, was because of her

---

[12]Ibid., 91.

firm belief that God would take care of her until her time came. "Lord," she would pray, "I'm going to hold steady on to you," and she expected Him not to let go. As she went about her work, she often sang of His faithfulness, songs that she composed and those that she had learned from childhood. One of her personal creations expressed her hope:

> Dark and thorny is the path,
> Where the pilgrim makes his way;
> But beyond this vale of sorrow
> Lie the fields of endless days.

In a letter to Sarah Bradford in June 1868, Harriet's dear Quaker friend Thomas Garrett wrote, "In truth, I never met with any person, of any color, who had more confidence in the voice of God, as spoken direct to her soul. She has frequently told me that she talked with God, and he talked with her every day of her life. . . ."[13]

---

[13]Charles L. Blockson, *The Underground Railroad* (New York: Prentice Hall Press, 1987), 171.

3

Yearning for Liberation

He was fun-loving, nice to look at, and free—"the only deeply physical love of her life."[1] They met sometime during the period that they worked for John Stewart, each on different terms—he a free man, Harriet a slave. The particulars of how and when they first became attracted to each other aren't entirely clear, but John Tubman knew an exceptional woman when he saw one.

John's family came from the western side of Cambridge, Maryland, where they had served for years at Lockerman's Manor, an estate overlooking the Choptank River. It was in his boyhood that John and his family were freed at the time of their master's death, as stipulated in his will. Like most free Southern blacks in the antebellum era, the Tubmans stuck to the countryside to make their living, mostly as farmhands and unskilled laborers.

It wasn't unusual for liberated African-Americans to work side-by-side with slaves. Of course, that presented some difficulties for the free workers, who car-

---

[1] Conrad, 32.

ried papers at all times to prove that they were emancipated. To Harriet Ross, with her lifelong yearning for liberation, John was especially attractive. Surely someone who could call his life his own would understand her own longing to be free. Even John suffered insult and injustice every time a white person automatically assumed that because he was black he must be a slave.

When Harriet and John Tubman got married, she was about twenty-three years old, well past the normal age when slaves—and whites for that matter—wed. Most slaves married in their mid-teen years, but during that period in her own life, Harriet was still recovering from her head injury. Moreover, many people thought that the incident had left her "simple," especially considering her frequent and unexpected sleeping spells that often made her mouth go slack. Anyone seeing her in such a state could not have been faulted for thinking she was mentally deficient, a misconception that Harriet didn't try to correct. In fact, she believed that it put her at an advantage; if she ever hoped to escape, the less bright her master thought she was, the better her chances for outwitting him. Nor did Harriet seem, for all her physical prowess, to be a good prospect for having children. It is likely, then, that her master gave his blessing when she fell in love with John Tubman. That he was free made little difference. Such "mixed marriages" often took place, as long as the couple understood that the slave partner was going to remain that way.

According to those who knew him, Tubman was a jokester, handsome, and charming—an easygoing man who, like Harriet, loved to sing. Besides his pleasing external qualities, Harriet was attracted to this man because he could read and write. She had a high regard for literacy, and because Tubman was both free and learned, he could help her in her own quest to gain freedom.

The details of Harriet and John's betrothal and wedding are sparse. They were joined in marriage sometime in 1844, and it is possible that they were united at a broomstick ceremony, like a majority of slaves, in which they would jump over a broomstick to seal their vows to each other. Whether this might have been different because John was free isn't apparent. Their marriage, however, would not have been legally recognized because Harriet was a slave, nor were they allowed to promise to be together *till death do us part*. In fact, the word *distance* may have been substituted for *death* because a slave owner had the right to sell any of his people at any time that he deemed necessary. For that reason, the admonition "What God has joined together, let no man put asunder" would also have been omitted from their wedding ceremony.

The Tubmans went to live in the same slave quarters in which Harriet had been residing, and as the years unfolded they remained childless. Although John was content enough with his fairly stable lot in life, Harriet burned within for the freedom her husband had enjoyed since childhood.

John didn't truly understand Harriet's unhappiness about being a slave. Whenever she mentioned running away together to make a new life for themselves in the North, he tried to discourage her. He wanted her to be as content with her lot in life as he was with his own. It even got to the point where John threatened to betray her if she tried to leave. His attitude broke her heart, but Harriet would not be deterred. If she couldn't live free, she reasoned, why live at all? She also came to believe that her family should have been freed years earlier but had been cheated by a lying master.

For a while Harriet had suspected, based on a story her mother told her from her youth, that if she could trace back far enough through legal records, she might be able to prove that her family should be free. Sometime in the late 1840s, Harriet paid a lawyer five dollars to trace the will of her mother's first master. Through his research, Harriet discovered that under the terms of the will, her mother, Harriet Greene at the time, was to serve her master's granddaughter, Mary Patterson, and later Mary's children. This arrangement was to continue until Mary died or Harriet Greene turned forty-five, whichever came first. Mary Patterson never married. In fact, she died shortly after the will was made, meaning that Harriet Greene should have gone free.

The details of how freedom was denied Old Rit are not clear, but the fact is that she remained in her deceitful master's service. When her daughter learned of this years later, she regarded it as a deliberate trick. This incident presented another opportunity for bitterness to put down roots in Harriet's spirit, but she would have none of it. When she told the story to Sarah Bradford, it was "without any mourning or lamenting over the wrong and the misery of it all, accepting it as the will of God, and, therefore, not to be rebelled against."[2] Although Harriet wasn't bitter, she did hope to use the information to right the wrong, except there wasn't time.

In 1849 her young master, the heir to Edward Brodas' plantation, died. Rumors started to fly immediately, leaving Harriet breathless. Through a slave

---

[2]Bradford, 129.

from another plantation, she heard that Dr. Thompson, who had acted as her master's guardian over the years, planned to cut some of his economic losses by getting rid of certain slaves. She and two of her brothers were to be sold to a Georgia slave trader. The very idea horrified Harriet, who had faced such an awful prospect fifteen years earlier, narrowly escaping when Edward Brodas died. Now, through another master's death, the possibility of being sold once again raised the terrifying likelihood that Harriet would be separated from the people she most loved, including her husband.

As she saw it, now was the time to escape to the North, to make a new home for herself and John where they could live as peacefully and free as God desired for His children. She would miss her parents and siblings terribly, and even her native eastern shore, but if she were free, she could come back for them when she was able so they could all be together again. Maybe now that Harriet was about to be sold away from him and the life they had made together, John would change his mind about going north. *Surely he'll be willing to go now*, she reasoned. *What was the alternative? How could he live without her?*

Unfortunately, John only became more adamant in his refusal to escape with his wife. It would be far too dangerous to try to run away, he said. He was content to live as he always had, even if it was in the shadow of white people who lorded their authority over him. What could he do to stop a slave sale once a master had made up his mind? How could one man hope to change or influence a centuries-old system? John had long ago accepted the South's established social order. Why couldn't Harriet?

Harriet could not because with every breath she

drew she craved the physical counterpart of the liberation the Lord had given her soul years earlier. Nor could she accept the status quo when she had been destined by God to free as many of her people as possible.

Without John's blessing—indeed, with his threats to expose her should she try to escape still burning in her ears—Harriet thought out her plan. She was ready to face any danger, including death. She told herself,

> There's two things I got a right to and these are Death and Liberty. One or the other I mean to have. . . . No one will take me back alive; I shall fight for my liberty, and when the time has come for me to go, the Lord will let them kill me.[3]

Harriet knew that she had to act quickly if she was going to make a successful escape. Otherwise the slave traders would carry her off to Georgia, and then fleeing to the North would be even more difficult. Suspecting that she was up to something and worried about his own safety, John tried to intimidate her into giving up her plan. He was going to notify the authorities the minute he discovered that she was missing. With great stealth, Harriet met secretly with the two brothers who also were going to be sold. They, too, were willing to go north with her.

On the night before their flight, in the summer of 1849, Harriet took the breakfast ashcake she had prepared for the following day's morning meal, along with a piece of salt herring, and wrapped them in a bandanna. She was excited about realizing her long-term dream of freedom, but she also felt sad about leaving

---

[3]Blockson, *The Underground Railroad*, 98.

the people who were so dear to her. She had to find
some way to say good-bye, one that wouldn't betray
her intentions. It would be too risky to tell everyone
that she and her brothers were going to escape, especially their emotional mother. Her father probably
would take the news coolly. He might try to talk his
children out of running away, but he would be calm
about it—nothing like Old Rit, who wasn't one to hold
back her feelings. Harriet feared that her mother's
storminess might give away the entire scheme. Instead of outright disclosure, Harriet decided to use an
old and familiar Negro spiritual that she often sang
while at work. Her friends would be able to read between its lines once they learned what she had done.

On that warm summer night, thick with the drones
of insects calling to one another, Harriet wandered,
seemingly idly, past the doors of her friends and family's quarters singing:

> I'm sorry, friends, to leave you,
> Farewell! oh, farewell!
> But I'll meet you in the morning,
> Farewell! oh, farewell!
>
> I'll meet you in the morning,
> When you reach the Promised Land;
> On the other side of Jordan,
> For I'm bound for the Promised Land.[4]

Then Harriet noticed that her master was standing at the gate of the big house. Although she felt a
little nervous, she knew she had to act as normally as
possible. As she passed by him with a nod, she continued singing her brave and meaningful tune. Years
after that pivotal night, Dr. Thompson told someone

4Bradford, 28.

how calm Harriet had looked, as if "a wave of trouble never rolled across her peaceful breast."[5] Little did he suspect at the time that "she was only quitting home, husband, father, mother, friends, to go out alone, friendless and penniless into the world."[6]

Before the next morning dawned, Harriet and her brothers had fled the plantation. Almost immediately, however, the enormity of what they were trying to accomplish with its terrible risks so scared the men that they turned back.

Harriet wanted no part of giving up. She was not going to be sold. She was going to live free or die. She continued on, completely alone. "Oh, dear Lord," she prayed, "I ain't got no friend but you. Come to my help, Lord, for I'm in trouble."

[5]Blockson, 119.
[6]Ibid.

4

Freedom

The legendary Underground Railroad that Harriet Tubman was about to take consisted of a variety of routes that slaves used on their way out of captivity. Some have said this secret system of fictional "trains" and nonexistent "tracks" was "one of history's finest symbols of the struggle against oppression" and that it "embodied the nation's leading principle: the quest for freedom."[1]

Harriet first heard of this mysterious network when she was a child growing up on Edward Brodas' plantation. She listened as other slaves spoke in guarded whispers about those who had run away and made it safely to the North, where they lived and moved freely, away from any master but the Lord God. Harriet's imagination and spirit stirred. She thought about the frequent dreams she had about the line that separated slave from free states. Then there were those strange white women who stretched out their welcoming arms to her from beyond that line, beckoning her to their land of green fields and beautiful

---

[1]*Underground Railroad* (Washington, D.C.: Division of Publications, National Park Service, 1998), 45–46.

flowers. But in her dreams she could never reach them. Something always caused her to fall before she could get to them. Harriet resolved that someday, somehow, she would find a way to cross over.

She was among a large number of slaves—possibly 100,000 by some accounts—who made it successfully past many formidable obstacles in a death-defying pursuit of freedom. No one knows for certain just how many blacks actually did try to escape, nor who made it and who didn't. Keeping records of those attempts was extremely dangerous to those who assisted runaway slaves. With few contemporary documents of the Underground Railroad, most of the accounts and information appeared years after the fact in the autobiographies and biographies of participants. Many stories, greatly embellished by reporters and aging abolitionists, appeared in the nation's newspapers and magazines after the Civil War and often were full of sensational stories that were nearly impossible to believe.

One man who did keep accurate and contemporary records, however, was a courageous Philadelphian named William Still. A free-born black, he kept a journal in which he made brief entries about each runaway who came seeking help at the offices of the General Vigilance Committee of Philadelphia, of which he was the director. This was, of course, a very risky thing for Still to do. The dangers were all the more apparent when abolitionist John Brown's papers and letters "with names and plans in full" (including many Underground Railroad references) were seized, right after Brown's doomed attempt to free southern slaves in October 1859.

Not wanting his own records to fall into enemy hands, Still began to exclude some of the more potentially damaging details of escapees and their stories, particularly who had helped them along the routes to the North. Still sent most of his books and papers away for safekeeping. He didn't stop taking down the stories of fugitive slaves' escapes, however. Instead, he began to write them on "loose slips of paper" that could be stuffed away quickly, easily, and in more than one hiding place.[2]

There had always been people willing to help slaves like Harriet Tubman escape; George Washington spoke of the difficulty he had in recovering a runaway slave at Valley Forge. In 1793 the United States Congress passed a fugitive slave statute. According to its provisions, owners could recapture their human property without so much as a warrant for their arrest. Afterward, the slave master or his representative had to go to court in the state in which the arrest had been made to obtain that court's permission to take the slave or slaves back home. If anyone was caught helping a slave run away, or interfering with the apprehension of one, a five-hundred dollar fine was levied against that party. Yet people continued to help slaves escape. The term "Underground Railroad" and the system that it involved didn't come into use, however, until actual trains on real railroads started to make an impact in the 1830s. Those who defied slavery employed railroad terminology as code words to describe their activities. There was, however, no nationally organized Underground Railroad. Most efforts at assisting runaways occurred more locally and often haphazardly.

Philadelphia, with its large Quaker and black populations, had what was probably the most vigorous

---

[2]Still, 531.

and organized of Underground Railroad stations.[3] Between 1830 and 1860, thousands of runaways were directed through that city along well-established and well-run routes. At its heart was William Still, who helped create a network of safe houses for fugitives and who also channeled them to other conductors along the routes farther to the North. His Vigilance Committee consisted largely of Philadelphia's black working class, of men and women who did the "grunt work" of the committee, providing food, shelter, and transportation for the runaways, as well as gathering and relaying important information.[4]

Circuit-riding preachers of the African Methodist Episcopal (A.M.E.) Church also played a crucial role in helping slaves elude capture. In fact, the most singularly important Underground Railroad station in Philadelphia was the Mother Bethel A.M.E. Church, founded in 1791 by Richard Allen, who was himself a former slave.[5]

If you were a slave on the run, the two most important elements in your bid to flee to and live successfully in the North were a reasonable escape route and a secure place to live once you reached your destination. An amazingly simple yet far-reaching system of signals and codes was used to assist the fugitives in this quest. For example, an American flag in a cast-iron statue's hand meant that it was safe for a slave to approach that house and seek help there. If the iron figure was that of a black man who held a lantern and wore a red jockey cap, the home was a "junc-

---

[3]*Underground Railroad*, NPS, 61.
[4]Ibid.
[5]This church, in which Harriet Tubman often took Communion, is standing on the oldest piece of property continuously owned by blacks in the United States.

tion," or stopover point. In addition, weather vanes that were positioned in certain directions also served as codes for runaways.

On the Underground Railroad, the use of riddles, passwords, handshakes, and other rituals of identification was widespread. For example, "small parcels" were children, and large ones were adults. To distinguish oneself as a fugitive slave in search of assistance, and to make sure that the place you had stopped at was indeed a safe haven, a conversation might go something like this: "You travel late, neighbor. It's a dark night. Shall I bring a lantern?" The hoped-for response was, "Don't bother, the North Star is bright," a reference to the means by which many slaves found their way to the North. Or the owner of the place might ask, "Who's there?" The answer: "A friend with friends," which was Harriet Tubman's own code.

Ferryboats on the Delaware Bay were often used to transport slaves across the water into Pennsylvania, and they identified themselves by using a blue light above a yellow light. Likewise, code language for members of the Underground Railroad often came from spirituals. It's little surprise they were one of Harriet's favorite means of communication.

Harriet loved to sing as she went about her daily routine. Because she often sang aloud, and since so many slaves knew the lyrics about Israel's sojourn in Egypt and the promise of eternal life, she could use them without drawing any suspicion. One of her favorites went:

Hail, oh hail, ye happy spirits,
Death no more shall make you fear,
Grief nor sorrow, pain nor anguish,

Shall no more distress you dear.

Around Him are ten thousand angels,
Always ready to obey command;
They are always hovering round you,
Till you reach the heavenly land.

Jesus, Jesus will go with you,
He will lead you to his throne;
He who died, has gone before you,
Trod the winepress all alone.

He whose thunders shake creation,
He who bids the planets roll;
He who rides upon the tempest,
And whose scepter sways the whole.

Dark and thorny is the pathway,
Where the pilgrim makes his ways;
But beyond this vale of sorrow,
Lie the fields of endless days.[6]

The dangers of being exposed and captured were very real along the Underground Railroad. Slave masters often used subversive decoys to lure their people back, as well as impostors who would pose as fellow runaways, then betray them. These would win the confidence of fair-skinned African-American women who were escaping, go on to marry them, and then sell them back to their masters for a reward. Too many times Underground Railroad agents were found brutally murdered.

Those harsh realities necessitated extreme vigilance and ingenuity. Stops that provided shelter for runaways employed hiding places for them, including secret rooms with trapdoors, attics and basements,

---

[6]Ibid.

hidden passages, caves, barns, and carriages with false bottoms. In extreme cases, a box might be shipped north with a slave inside. The most famous incident of this nature happened in 1848 when Henry Brown of Richmond had himself sent to Philadelphia in a crate. At one point during his remarkable journey, Brown spent several hours on his head. His escapade earned him the nickname "Box Brown," and he became a popular speaker on the anti-slavery lecture circuit. Sometimes black undertakers even helped slaves escape in well-ventilated coffins.

At one Philadelphia home, a Quaker family that was secretly harboring fugitive slaves received a surprise visit from the local sheriff one evening. They put off his search by saying that they were about to pray, then asked him to join them. The runaways' only recourse was to rush upstairs as quietly as possible. Then they crawled onto the sloping roof and clung to it for dear life while the sheriff finally searched the house.

Running away from one's owner was an extremely dangerous affair. You could never be sure whom you could trust, and threats of betrayal and discovery were ever-present. One faced extremes in weather and traveling conditions, in addition to hunger, exposure, illness, and well-trained hunting dogs that ruthlessly pursued their human prey. Those who were captured often faced draconian punishments, including branding, whipping, and even maiming and death.

In the southern states, whites or free blacks who were caught helping fugitives faced huge fines, imprisonment, or even hard labor. Any white person was permitted to stop any black for any reason and demand to see a travel pass or emancipation papers. Southerners tended to believe that any black on the roads had to be up to no good. If the person failed to produce those items, he or she could be hauled off to jail for a full investigation.

A white Kentucky man named Calvin Fairbanks went to jail twice, serving a total of sixteen years for helping a family escape to Canada. Charles Torrey, a conductor on the Underground Railroad, aided roughly four hundred slaves before his arrest. He subsequently died of tuberculosis in a dismal Baltimore prison. In Maryland, where the novel *Uncle Tom's Cabin* was banned, one black minister was sentenced to ten years in prison because he had a copy of it in his possession. Even in the free North, a person who helped runaway slaves might not fare much better. In Massachusetts, sea Captain Jonathan Walker hid four slaves on his ship. When he was caught, the authorities branded his right hand with "S.S." for "slave stealer." He also served eight months in jail and had to compensate the slaveholders for their losses.[7]

In 1850 Congress passed an updated Fugitive Slave Act, written by Henry Clay, the great statesman from Kentucky. It was part of the Compromise of 1850, in which sectional tensions between the North and South were addressed, particularly whether slavery was to be permitted in new territories to the West. According to the new version of the law, persons who impeded the retrieval of a slave, or who helped one escape, would be subject to a maximum fine of one thousand dollars and six months in prison. The law also stipulated that a federal commissioner could summon a posse to recover a runaway slave and that it could impress anyone in its service. If a person refused, he or she could face fines or imprisonment.

---

[7]Bradford, 36–37.

There also would be no recourse to trial by jury for the fugitive slave. Since descriptions of them tended to be general and often downright vague, any black who bore even a slight resemblance to a known runaway could find himself in serious jeopardy.[8] Such were "the years of terror of the Fugitive Slave Law."[9]

It is no wonder that within thirty-six hours of passage of that Act, forty blacks fled from Massachusetts to Canada. Britain had abolished slavery throughout its Empire in 1833, and Queen Victoria flatly refused to allow U.S. officials to enter her realm to reclaim runaway slaves. Roughly twenty thousand blacks found their way across the border to Canada by the end of the Civil War.[10] As a result of the tougher law, hundreds of free blacks were kidnapped, and protection groups began to form among African-American communities.

Northerners were especially incensed that the expanded law required those who lived in free states to be at the service of anyone who was searching for runaways. Suddenly, they could be forced to be agents of a system that many of them loathed, or else be fined or sent to jail.[11] While some Northerners had been indifferent toward slavery before 1850 and others had viewed most abolitionists as dangerous extremists, afterward many came to approve of moderate efforts to rid the country of slavery. They began to see that emancipation was a moral issue that impacted the nation at large. In addition, most Northerners came to admire the courage of runaways and those who endangered themselves by assisting them. They saw

---

[8]NPS, 63.
[9]Ibid., 66.
[10]Bradford, ix.
[11]Conrad, 44.

those people as fighting for freedom, which was supposed to define the very nature of the United States.[12]

Harriet Tubman's escape in 1849 and her later work as a conductor brought her into this frightening quagmire. This one slave woman, who was quite alone, with nothing to commend her in a worldly sense, was about to defy a ruthless, but legal, system. And yet, strengthened by her God, she would make foolish the wisdom of a society that stood against her people.

---

[12]NPS, 68.

5

Stranger in a Strange Land

Like her Old Testament counterpart, Harriet "Moses" Tubman led many of her people out of slavery and into the Promised Land, but she was also like him in another respect. Before God used both Moses and Harriet, He first took them away from all that they had once known and loved. That prospect was enough to make Harriet's two brothers turn and flee in terror, preferring "the devil they knew." But for Harriet, freedom was worth paying any price, bearing any burden. She would not wait for someone to grant it to her, and she did not intend to be deceived by a master, as her mother had been.

Harriet had heard of two large cities where blacks lived free: Philadelphia and New York. She made up her mind to get to one or the other in spite of desperate handicaps—she was penniless and a fugitive of the law. She had no maps, no compass. Her food supply consisted of the paltry snack she had taken from her cabin. She had never been taught to read or write. There was no one to encourage or support her. Even her husband would sound the alarm the minute he realized that she had run away.

Nevertheless, there was at least some balm in Gilead in the form of a woman who had once offered to help Harriet if she ever decided to break away. She had met the white woman, a Quaker named Miss Parsons, while working in the fields one day.[1] The woman had stopped to exchange greetings with Harriet and became curious about the origin of the scar on the slave's forehead. Miss Parsons was clearly moved by the story. She told Harriet about her farm in nearby Bucktown and that "if you ever need any help, let me know." It was a cryptic invitation. Harriet wasn't entirely sure what Miss Parsons could do for her, but the woman was her only human consolation at the time she escaped.

That Harriet trusted Miss Parsons at all is extraordinary in and of itself. Until that time, whites had given her few reasons to believe in their goodwill. She was soon to discover, however, just how many decent white people were out there in the wider world, people who had deep convictions against slavery and who were poised to help her win her precious freedom in any way they could.

Harriet and her brothers had left in the early morning hours, and after the men had turned back, she raced on to Miss Parsons' farm. She found it just as the woman had described it. Fortunately, Miss Parsons remembered Harriet and was glad that she had come for help. This association was Harriet's first encounter with the Underground Railroad. After eating a nourishing meal, she listened as the Quaker told her about two other "stops" on the mythical railroad and

---

[1]Harriet Tubman's great-niece, Mariline Wilkins, believes the woman's name, Miss Parsons, was a code she used for her Underground Railroad activities.

the people who would help her as she made her way north.

Harriet moved quickly and furtively that night when it was safer to travel, following the bank of the Choptank River. She always kept the North Star to the front and left of her. When she couldn't find it among the clouds, she would find her direction by feeling for moss that grew on the north side of trees.

In the morning Harriet finally arrived at the first house to which Miss Parsons had directed her. She became frightened, however, when the couple she met there gave her a broom and told her to start sweeping outside. Was it possible that Miss Parsons had tricked her? Was this some kind of trap? That seemed too out of character for the gentle but determined Quaker. She wasn't the betraying kind. Later that day, the man of the house relieved Harriet's fears when he loaded his wagon with produce and quietly directed her to scoot down low and hide under it. Then he covered her with blankets and got behind the reins. Although she was nervous as he started down the road, she was so tired that she quickly fell asleep to the lulling sounds of the wheels against the road and the rhythmic *clip-clop* of the horse's hooves.

At the next stop along the Underground Railroad, Harriet received food and more information for her journey, then continued on her way, her face resolutely set toward the North. She continued along the river, walking at night, staying off the main roads where she was more likely to be discovered. When she could follow the water no longer, Harriet kept on a northeasterly course toward Camden, Delaware, where Ezekiel Hunn, a farmer who was active in the Underground Railroad, provided food and information about her next stops. She had made it past one state line—only one remained.

From Camden, Harriet journeyed to Middletown, where Ezekiel's brother, John, received her into his home, which was also a station. She ventured next to New Castle, then on to Wilmington. That is where she first came into contact with an extraordinary man who would become her fearless partner in rescuing slaves, as well as her devoted and lifelong friend.

Born in Philadelphia in 1789, Thomas Garrett was a Quaker shoe salesman who harbored strong anti-slavery convictions. When he moved to nearby Wilmington, Delaware, in 1822, he started hiding runaways in the rooms above his store. During the next forty years, Garrett assisted between twenty-five hundred and three thousand slaves, giving them food, shelter, money, and of course, plenty of shoes. At one point toward the end of his "career," the authorities fined Garrett so heavily for assisting slave refugees that he lost everything. At the age of sixty, he had to start all over again. Once he earned back some of his earlier prosperity, however, he was arrested and fined again for continuing to assist runaways. The incredulous judge at his trial told him, "Garrett, let this be a lesson to you, not to interfere hereafter with the cause of justice by helping runaway negroes."

Garrett was not persuaded. He responded in true Quaker form, "Judge, thee hasn't left me a dollar, but I wish to say to thee, and to all in this court room, that if anyone knows of a fugitive who wants a shelter, and a friend, send him to Thomas Garrett, and he will befriend him!"[2] It was said of him that "not even Luther before the Council at Worms was grander than this

---

[2]Bradford, 53–54.

brave old man in his unswerving adherence to principle."[3]

During the course of her courageous escape, Harriet had been rowed up the Choptank and hidden in the attic of a Quaker homestead. She spent several days in the haystack of a German immigrant and in a free black family's storage hole for potatoes to elude any pursuers. Now it was time for one more wagon ride north. From there she walked across the Pennsylvania line. Her first impression of freedom both intoxicated and awed Harriet. She said, "I looked at my hands to see if I was the same person, now that I was free. There was such a glory over everything. The sun came up like gold through the trees and over the fields, and I felt like I was in Heaven."[4]

Although this was the end of Harriet's journey to liberty, she was just at the beginning of many decisions and difficulties. Where would she live? What kind of job would she find? Would she make new friends? Whom could she trust? Looking back in her later years, she described how she felt at that time:

> I knew of a man who was sent to the State Prison for twenty-five years. All these years he was always thinking of his home, and counting by years, months, and days, the time till he should be free, and see his family and friends once more. The years roll on, the time of imprisonment is over, the man is free. He leaves the prison gates, he makes his way to his old home, but his old home is not there. The house in which he had dwelt in his childhood had been torn down, and a new one had been put up in its place; his family

[3]Ibid.
[4]Rebecca Price Janney, *Great Women in American History* (Camp Hill, Pa.: Horizon Books, 1996), 228.

were gone, their very name was forgotten, there was no one to take him by the hand to welcome him back to life.

So it was with me. I had crossed the line of which I had so long been dreaming. I was free; but there was no one to welcome me to the land of freedom, I was a stranger in a strange land, and my home after all was down in the old cabin quarter, with the old folks, and my brothers and sisters.[5]

For Harriet it was time not to rest and relax but to start working toward the attainment of her lifelong goal—to be used by God to set many of her captive people free. She said,

But to this solemn resolution I came; I was free, and they should be free also; I would make a home for them in the North, and the Lord helping me, I would bring them all there. Oh, how I prayed then, lying all alone on the cold, damp ground; "Oh, dear Lord," I said, "I ain't got no friend but you. Come to my help, Lord, for I'm in trouble!"[6]

Shortly after her arrival in Philadelphia, Harriet met William Still, who would become a vital part of that venture. Through Still's Philadelphia Vigilance Committee, Harriet found places to live and to work, and she learned more about the activities of the Underground Railroad that had helped her escape. In fact, she spent most of her evenings at the Vigilance Committee offices.

During Harriet's first year in the North, she had several jobs, mostly as a laundress, cleaning woman, cook, and seamstress at hotels and in clubhouses.

---

[5]Bradford, 31–32.
[6]Ibid.

Harriet so enjoyed her freedom to choose her own work and bosses that she moved a lot in those initial months. Because of her dogged determination to rescue her family, she lived frugally, laying aside most of her wages for that purpose.

Harriet Tubman was determined that all blacks should be free. In spite of her formidable journey north, "No fear of the lash, the bloodhound, or the fiery stake, could divert her from her self-imposed task of leading as many as possible of her people 'from the land of Egypt, from the house of bondage.' "[7] It wasn't enough to have moral convictions against slavery. Harriet believed such convictions were only good if a person acted on them. She was, for her part, willing to do whatever it took.

[7]Ibid., 11.

6

All Aboard!

When God told Moses to go before Pharaoh and demand that he let the Israelites go, it seems that Moses thought the Lord had made a mistake. Trembling near the burning bush, Moses offered up any number of excuses to the Lord. Who was he, after all, to go before the world's most powerful man and demand such a thing? God's response: "I will be with you." Then Moses pointed out that the Israelites would wonder just who this God was anyway. When the Lord revealed His name, however, Moses still wasn't satisfied. The Israelites never would believe that God actually had appeared to him. The Lord, therefore, gave him the ability to perform wondrous signs as proof. Moses still wasn't convinced that he was the right man for the job, so he told God about his poor speaking skills, as if He didn't know. The Lord remained adamant. He had chosen Moses to appear before Pharaoh, and it was Moses who would go.

Such reluctance to fulfill her own divine calling never seems to have occurred to Harriet Tubman, in spite of the extraordinary odds against her. In that respect, she was less like Moses and more like David, the shepherd youth who took on the Philistine giant, Goliath. Standing before the titan, David said, "You come against me with sword and spear and javelin, but I come against you in the name of the Lord Almighty, the God of the armies of Israel, whom you have defied" (1 Sam. 17:45). In that same Name, Harriet would find all her needs met, all her fears relieved. She had complete confidence in God's desire and ability to help her in all ways. William Still said of her,

> In point of courage, shrewdness and disinterested exertion to rescue her fellowmen, by making personal visits into Maryland among the slaves, she was without her equal. . . . It is obvious enough . . . that her success in going into Maryland as she did, was attributable to her adventurous spirit and utter disregard of consequences. Her like, it is probable, was never known before or since.[1]

Harriet's first test of courage and faith as an Underground Railroad conductor came in December 1850 when she received word that one of her sisters, her brother-in-law, and their two children had made it as far as Baltimore in their own escape attempt. Harriet went after them and led the group safely back to Philadelphia. A few months later she once again slipped across the Mason-Dixon Line that ran between Maryland and Pennsylvania to rescue one of her brothers and two other men.

As she started to go back on a regular basis, Har-

---

[1]Judith Nies, *Seven Women: Portraits From the American Radical Tradition* (New York: Viking Press, 1977), 43.

riet developed certain patterns. She considered it best to lead out the runaways on a Saturday night when slaves were permitted by their masters to visit one another. Since they weren't due back until Monday morning, and it might take a master and his helpers until Tuesday to put up notices of any who had escaped, Harriet and her group could get a significant head start on any pursuers. In addition, she liked to go in the harshness of winter when people spent more time indoors, reducing opportunities for discovery.

Harriet's rescue methods likely varied according to the situation. When she arrived in the general vicinity of the slaves who would be going north with her, she usually didn't present herself directly to them because that would be far too risky. Instead, she would send someone else to inform them that Moses had come to deliver them. Their point of rendezvous was often within eight to ten miles of the plantation. At other times, Harriet would appear suddenly and mysteriously "at the door of one of the cabins on a plantation, where a trembling band of fugitives, forewarned as to time and place, were anxiously awaiting their deliverer."[2]

Harriet thought it necessary to limit the number of slaves she would assist during any one trip according to how well she could provide for them in all respects. Nevertheless, she would give directions to those who wanted to escape at that time, but for whom she didn't have enough resources. Sometimes she escorted fugitives as far as Philadelphia or New York, leaving the people in other capable hands before venturing back into Maryland to rescue others.

Although Harriet was heroic, she was not reckless

---

[2]Bradford, 32.

by any stretch of the imagination. She knew that many Underground Railroad conductors such as herself had been caught, imprisoned, and/or hanged for their offenses. She once told her friend Thomas Garrett that she ventured only where God sent her, and she trusted Him to keep her safe until His work for her was complete.

One thing Harriet had to guard against was the infiltrators and informers who would pose as runaways for the opportunity to betray her and reap a generous reward. Her fear of bounty hunters was another reason that she always carried a pistol (and sometimes required others assisting her to do so) and wouldn't permit anyone to turn back once they had started to escape. A reporter once asked if she would ever shoot a man who would desert. She told him, "Yes. . . . Do you think I'd let so many die, just for one coward man?"[3] Harriet believed that if a person was weak enough to quit, he certainly would give out under duress, endangering that rescue mission and others to come.

"One time a man gave out the second night," Harriet recalled. "His feet were sore and swollen, he couldn't go any farther; he'd rather go back." Harriet's attempts to soothe his fears were in vain; there was just one thing left to do. She hadn't lost a single passenger yet, and she wasn't about to now. "I told the boys to get their guns ready, and shoot him," she said. "They'd have done it in a minute; but when he heard that, he jumped right up and went on as well as anybody."[4]

William Still said of her determination not to let anyone defect:

[3]Conrad, 77.
[4]Blockson, *The Underground Railroad*, 121.

After having once enlisted, "they had to go through or die." Of course Harriet was supreme, and her followers generally had full faith in her, and would back up any word she might utter. So when she said to them that "a live runaway could do great harm by going back, but that a dead one could tell no secrets," she was sure to have obedience. . . . She would not suffer one of her party to whimper once about "giving out and going back," however wearied they might be from hard travel day and night. She had a very short and pointed rule or law of her own, which implied death to any who talked of giving out and going back. Thus, in an emergency she would give all to understand that "times were very critical and therefore no foolishness would be indulged in on the road." That several who were rather weak-kneed and faint-hearted were greatly invigorated by Harriet's blunt and positive manner and threat of extreme measures, there could be no doubt.[5]

Harriet was also concerned about the amount of noise that babies on the journey might make, which easily could have jeopardized their position. In order to protect her fugitives and herself, she used either opium, paregoric, or laudanum—whatever drug was available—to keep infants quiet.

During one trip in particular, Harriet's faith and ingenuity were tested when she went to a village market for a pair of chickens. As she passed through the area, she suddenly saw her former master, Dr. Thompson. Harriet took immediate precautions to disguise herself. First, she pulled her sunbonnet down low and assumed the walk of an elderly, stooped woman. Just as quickly, she untied the string around the chickens'

---

[5]Still, 297.

legs. When the birds started clucking and banging around the street, Harriet went into full acting mode, shuffling as quickly as an elderly person could in an "exasperated" attempt to gather the birds. Thompson chuckled at the playful scene, having no idea how seriously he was being duped.[6]

One thing that might have hindered Harriet's mission was her inability to read or write. In fact, most southern slaves were illiterate as a means to keep them subservient and unable to function independently of their masters. Harriet was innately intelligent, however, and when she lacked some aptitude or asset, she learned to adapt in other ways. For example, she could detect whether an Underground Railroad worker she had not previously met was authentic by showing the person daguerreotypes of mutual abolitionist friends. If the new person identified them from the pictures, he or she was to be trusted.

Harriet often used songs to communicate information to the slaves. Sometimes she would have to leave her group to get supplies or to gather intelligence, for example. Upon her return, she would alert her band that it was time to go by singing a spiritual whose words contained a double meaning. The following one meant that it was time—and safe—to come out of hiding.

> Oh go down, Moses,
> Way down into Egypt's land;
> Tell old Pharaoh,
> Let my people go.
>
> Ol' Pharaoh said he would go 'cross;
> Let my people go,

---

[6]Bradford, 34–35.

And don't get lost in the wilderness.
Let my people go.

Oh go down, Moses,
Way down into Egypt's land;
Tell old Pharaoh,
Let my people go.

You may hinder me here,
But you can't up there;
Let my people go.
He sits in the Heaven
And answers prayer.
Let my people go!

Oh go down, Moses,
Way down into Egypt's land;
Tell old Pharaoh,
Let my people go.[7]

If it was too dangerous for the runaways to come
out of hiding just then, Harriet would add a stanza.
She often used the following one.

Moses, go down in Egypt;
Tell old Pharaoh, let me go;
Hadn't been for Adam's fall,
Shouldn't 'ave to 'ave died at all.[8]

Another method that Harriet used to protect her
fugitives was to hire a man to find out who was putting
up "Wanted" posters of her and the escaped slaves.
Then he would follow the person putting up the fliers
and tear them down as quickly as they went up.

The route Harriet took followed an established and
mostly predictable pattern, one that offered a degree

---

[7]Ibid., 37–38.
[8]Conrad, 77.

of security. Once she had moved her slaves safely through Maryland, she made several stops with them in Delaware. The customary last one was at the Wilmington business of Thomas Garrett, who always received her gladly. He would present her and each of her group with a much-needed pair of sturdy shoes, in addition to providing ample food and shelter for however long they needed to stay.

From there Harriet would sometimes take a steamboat, traveling on a certificate given to her by one of the captains that identified her as a free resident of Philadelphia. Although the pass gave her greater latitude, one time a clerk wouldn't sell her tickets in spite of it. Harriet became alert and suspicious, her runaways, frightened. Although she, too, was upset by the predicament and the possibility of being captured, Harriet went off by herself for a few minutes of prayer. Recalling the incident many years later, she said, "I drew in my breath and I sent it out to the Lord, but that was all I could say; and then again, and then a third time, and just then I felt a touch on my shoulder, and looked round, and the clerk said, 'Here's your tickets.' "[9]

When they arrived in Philadelphia at last, Harriet's people would tell their stories to chronicler William Still before heading on to New York City. There they would visit the Anti-Slavery Society offices where Harriet would visit with another dear friend, Oliver Johnson. Albany was the next stop, then Rochester, where Harriet frequently received assistance from Frederick Douglass and his wife, Ann. At other times she would stay at the A.M.E. Zion Church at Spring and Favor Streets, or with the Anthony, Bloss,

---

[9]Blockson, 122.

or Porter families, who willingly assisted her and her fatigued companions. Sometimes when in New York, she would go to abolitionist Gerrit Smith's large estate, where it was easy to find hiding places. The cherished final stop was St. Catherines in Ontario, Canada, where she would stay with her newly freed friends for several months, helping them get started materially and spiritually in their new lives.

For all of Harriet's success on the Underground Railroad, she did fail at bringing out one of the dearest people in the world to her. Ever since her own escape in 1849, she had dreamed of returning for her husband. She hoped that John had become so lonely for her that he would willingly go north just to be with her. In the fall of 1851, on her third trip to Maryland, wearing a man's suit and an old felt hat to avoid detection, Harriet ventured back to the old Brodas plantation for her sweetheart. According to one obviously fabricated account, when John opened his door, he stared at Harriet, dumbfounded. She held out her hands to him and smiled. "It's Harriet," she said. "I've come back for you, John." Just then a young, slim, and pretty woman came to see what was going on. It was Caroline, John's new wife.

Harriet provided her own version of the incident during an interview that was written up in 1863 in both *The Commonwealth* and the *Freeman's Record*. She said that when she neared the slave quarters, she sent word to John where she was staying and how he could find her. (One reason for her caution might have been that a local militia was patroling the area, on the lookout for suspicious-looking blacks.)

When John told the intermediary that he didn't want to see her, Harriet said at first she didn't care what the master might do to her, she wanted "to see her old man once more." Realizing the foolishness of such a move, however, she decided that if John could do without her, she would just go ahead and do without him. It was a turning point in her life. From then on, she would dedicate herself even more completely to the work of freeing her enslaved people. She quickly gathered a group of eleven slaves, including another brother and his family, and began the fifteen hundred-mile trip to Canada.[10]

That winter was a particularly cold one, especially for people who had never experienced such a season. The newly freed blacks earned their living by chopping wood as they endured frostbite. There never seemed to be enough to eat. Harriet spent the brutally cold months not resting from her labors but busily organizing collections of food and clothing, in addition to finding jobs and housing for her people. It wasn't enough to lead them out of Egypt; she wanted to give them a firm footing in the Promised Land as well.

> Rapidly she was building a mansion for freedom, and her legend was growing. Like Paul Bunyan who swung an axe and felled a forest, and black John Henry who could outdrill the steam engine, such was Harriet, who, when she took one step, straddled all of the states and placed a foot in another country! Only she was real and no myth! And a woman, something new in the lore of giant life![11]

Harriet's fellow abolitionist Oliver Johnson echoed those sentiments.

---

[10]The two brothers who were to have been sold along with Harriet to a Georgia slave trader remained in Maryland until they, too, escaped.

[11]Conrad, 47–48.

Her shrewdness in planning the escape of slaves, her skill in avoiding arrest, her courage in every emergency, and her willingness to endure hardship and face any danger for the sake of her poor followers was phenomenal.[12]

---

[12]Bradford, 8.

7

Wanted: Dead or Alive

Harriet Tubman faced great risks when she returned time after time to the South on her missions of redemption. The Fugitive Slave Act of 1850 made her dangerous work even more precarious because it gave anyone anywhere the authority to turn over a black who was even suspected of being a runaway. It was like being guilty until proven innocent. Then there was the rage that Southern slave owners harbored toward Harriet because she was stealing their "property" right out from under their eyes.

Harriet may have been "Moses" to her people and to abolitionists, but to her enemies she was a blight that had to be eliminated. Large rewards were posted for her capture—dead or alive. At one point, they totaled forty thousand dollars—the cost of several adult slaves in their prime. It may have been the highest price ever placed on a woman's head. God protected her from arrest on numerous occasions, however. One time Harriet sat outside a store quietly eating ice cream when a man came by and nailed up a "Wanted" poster for her capture. Not realizing who she was, the man turned to her and said, "If you see this nigger wench, you've got forty thousand dollars."

Harriet's sleep disorder also presented her with grave challenges. What would happen if she fell asleep at a critical point on a trip north? What if a frightened slave took advantage of that opportunity to leave the group and go back, or a slave hunter found her just at that time?

In spite of the personal hazards she faced, the lonely excursions back to "Egypt," the forfeiture of any kind of normal family life, and the bruising punishment her body sustained on every trip, Harriet persevered. She was determined to rescue every slave she could who desired to leave the South with her.

One of them was a tall, powerfully built man known to history only as "Joe." He got on board Harriet's freedom train on its seventh or eighth trip. His master had hired Joe out to another planter, and Joe had stayed there for six years. He did such a good job that it became unnecessary to hire an overseer. The planter valued Joe's work so highly that he finally purchased the slave at a high price—a thousand dollars down and a thousand more to be paid at a specified later date.

The following morning while Joe was at breakfast, the planter, sitting atop a horse with rawhide in hand, called for him to come out and submit to a whipping. The request startled Joe. He had seen his new master beat another slave mercilessly just a few days earlier out in the fields, and his initial reaction was to resist somehow. Then again, if he put up a fuss physically, Joe figured he might be even worse off than if he simply acquiesced. Either way, it seemed he would come up the loser in the situation. As he stood in the doorway of his cabin, Joe decided to at least try to plead his case.

"Master, haven't I always been faithful to you?" he asked. "Haven't I worked through sun and rain, early in the morning and late at night? Haven't I saved you an overseer by doing his work? Have you anything to complain against me?" Joe waited tensely for the response.

The planter admitted that he had no complaints against Joe and that he had always worked well, but then he explained his rationale for wanting to whip him. "You belong to me now," he said. "You're my nigger, and the first lesson my niggers have to learn is that I am master and they belong to me, and are never to resist anything I order them to do. So I always begin by giving them a good licking. Now strip and take it."[1]

With other slaves peeking out from their cabins in fear and curiosity, Joe stripped and took the lash. As the whip tore open his back, though, he made up his mind never to suffer anything like it again. As quickly as he could manage it, Joe and his brother, William, stole away by night on a boat and rowed down the Choptank River to Old Ben Ross's cabin. There he told Harriet's father, "Next time Moses comes, let me know." In the meantime, he and his brother would hide themselves as best they could nearby. In fact, Harriet did arrive not long after that clandestine visit, and she whisked away Joe, William, and several others who were to join her for that journey to the Promised Land.

By day the group huddled together in potato holes, where they sometimes could hear their pursuers pass within feet of where they hid quietly, holding their

---

[1]Bradford, 40–41.

breath, saying their prayers. Other operators along the Underground Railroad disguised the band of fugitives as they passed from one safe haven to another. At one place Harriet's company had to break up in order to take various means of transportation to their destination; they couldn't be accommodated all at once. Then they rendezvoused at the home of Sam Greene, a helper who was later to be apprehended and imprisoned for ten years, not because he had assisted them, but because the authorities found a copy of *Uncle Tom's Cabin* in his house.

The journey was an especially difficult one. Slave hunters were out en masse trying to win the huge rewards that had been offered not only for Harriet's arrest, but for Joe's as well. The bounty for his capture had escalated from a thousand dollars to two thousand dollars because his new master needed his services so badly. Their situation grew especially tense as the group approached the Wilmington Bridge. There, Harriet learned through a friend that "the advertisements were up." Policemen were guarding the span just waiting for her and her fugitives. She quickly sent members of the group to various Underground Railroad homes in the vicinity until she could figure out what to do next. They had to make it across that bridge, but how?

For advice she turned to her reliable Quaker friend, Thomas Garrett. He had always been available to her in the past, and this time he came up with more than shoes. He developed a brilliant strategy. He contacted a team of bricklayers from nearby Pennsylvania and asked them to bring two wagons into Wilmington across the bridge, seemingly to work at a job by day. Then when they returned to the Quaker State at night, they'd hide the runaways on the bottom of the wagons and cover them with their supplies and blankets.

As the vehicles rattled across the bridge that evening, the hearts of its concealed passengers thumped wildly under the bricks and the blankets. Would the wagons be searched like so many others were? Would they be apprehended and thrown into jail? Was this to be the end of the line for Harriet? How they rejoiced when the authorities guarding the bridge waved them past! Quietly, in their hearts, they also praised God for His deliverance.

When they reached the office of the New York Anti-Slavery Society a few days later, however, Joe became deeply distressed when Oliver Johnson greeted him. "Well, Joe," he said, "I am glad to see the man who is worth two thousand dollars to his master."[2] The slave regarded him with a puzzled expression. How could Johnson know who he was? They'd never met before. Johnson answered his unspoken question by showing Joe the "Wanted" poster with a drawing of him. He told the dispirited man, "The description is so close that no one could mistake it."[3] From then on, Joe despaired of ever reaching Canada. Surely someone would recognize him along the way and return him to his miserable master.

For the rest of the three hundred-mile journey to the U.S.-Canada border at Niagara Falls, most of it spent in railcars, Joe acted restive and moody. He continually brooded about the horrid things that would happen to him if he was sent back. Harriet did her best to encourage him, assuring him that, according to one of her favorite expressions, the Lord had been

[2] Ibid., 46.
[3] Ibid.

with them in six troubles; He wouldn't desert them in the seventh. It didn't work. "From that time," she said, "Joe was silent. He talked no more. He sang no more. He sat with his head on his hand, and nobody could arouse him, nor make him take any interest in anything."[4]

At long last the suspension bridge came into view, and Canada lay invitingly on the other side. Harriet knew that until they reached the center of the bridge, where the United States ended and Canada began, they still weren't safe. The rest of the group didn't know this, though, and all but Joe were filled with ecstasy as they exclaimed over the magnificent Niagara Falls. They were about to be free, and they broke into song as the other train passengers watched and smiled:

> I'm on the way to Canada,
> That cold and dreary land,
> The sad effects of slavery,
> I can't no longer stand;
> I've served my Master all my days,
> Without a dime reward,
> And now I'm forced to run away.
> To flee the lash, abroad;
>
> Farewell, old Master,
> Don't think hard of me,
> I'm traveling on to Canada,
> Where all the slaves are free.
>
> The hounds are baying on my track,
> Old Master comes behind,
> Resolved that he will bring me back,
> Before I cross the line;

---

[4] Ibid., 48.

I'm now embarked for yonder shore,
Where a man's a man by law,
The iron horse will bear me over,
To shake the lion's paw;

Oh, righteous Father,
Wilt thou not pity me,
And help me on to Canada,
Where all the slaves are free.

Oh I heard Queen Victoria say,
That if we would forsake
Our native land of slavery,
And come across the lake;
That she was standing on the shore,
With arms extended wide,
To give us all a peaceful home,
Beyond the rolling tide;

Farewell, old Master,
Don't think hard of me,
I'm traveling on to Canada,
Where all the slaves are free.[5]

Joe, sitting with his head on his hands, was so engrossed in fear that he was oblivious to the joyful scene. When the train made it to the center of the bridge and crossed over the Canadian border, however, Harriet sprang to Joe's side of the train and shook him hard. "Joe! You've shaken the lion's paw!" she cried. He looked up at her with disbelieving eyes at first. "Joe!" she shouted, "You're in Queen Victoria's dominions! You're a free man!" From that moment, Joe was quite literally transformed. He raised his hands to heaven, and with tears coursing down his face, started shouting and singing:

---

[5]Ibid., 49–50.

Glory to God and Jesus too,
One more soul got safe;
Oh, go and carry the news,
One more soul got safe.[6]

A crowd of white women and men who had felt concern for Joe during his wretched train trip quickly surrounded him, rejoicing in his freedom. One woman handed him an elegant handkerchief to wipe away his abundant tears. As he did so, Joe exclaimed, "Thank the Lord! There's only one more journey for me now, and that's to Heaven!" After the conductor, Joe was the first one off the train.

The trip was another example of how Harriet didn't brood over life's "what if's." She had entrusted her mission and her life to the Lord, and she believed with all that was in her that He would take care of her until it was time to take her to her heavenly home. When that happened, she would revel in God's presence. There really was, in her mind, nothing to worry about. She was trusting in God's mercies no matter what.

On one occasion, Harriet was leading out nearly a dozen captives, including two babies, when the sound of barking dogs hot on their trail prompted her to lead the slaves into a frigid stream. There the searching animals wouldn't be able to pick up their scent.

At dawn she took the numbed and frightened runaways to the house of a black man who had helped her during other rescues. She approached the door as her group huddled tensely in the street, but when she knocked, her friend did not answer. Instead, an irate white man raised a window from an upper story and narrowed his eyes at the scene below him. He asked

---

[6]Ibid., 51.

suspiciously, "Who are you? What do you want?" Harriet inquired about her friend, but he wasn't there. He'd been forced to leave, the man explained, for "harboring niggers."

The Lord prompted Harriet to take the fugitives outside of town to a little island in the middle of a swamp with tall, foul-smelling grass. Holding the infants, who were well-drugged to keep them resting quietly, Harriet charged ahead of the others into the murky water. "We're going to lie here in the wet grass and pray," she told them. Normally she would have left them there while she went in search of supplies, but this time she didn't dare. The white man had probably alerted the local slave catchers.

Just after sundown, a man dressed as a Quaker and muttering to himself passed by the disagreeable swamp. Harriet immediately perked up to see what he was up to. Sure enough, when she inclined her head and listened closely to what he was saying, she could tell that he was speaking to her. "My wagon stands in the barnyard of the next farm across the way," he murmured. "The horse is in the stable, and the harness hangs on a nail." Help had come.

As soon as Harriet believed it was safe to leave, she waded out of the bog and hurried to the area of which the man had spoken. Just like he said, there was a wagon, and it contained a large quantity of food. Harriet took her people in the vehicle to the next town, where a Quaker whom she knew took charge of the horse and wagon. Harriet never knew how the first man had heard about their plight, but she didn't question it. Sarah Bradford said, "These sudden deliverances never seemed to strike her as at all strange or mysterious; her prayer was the prayer of faith, and she expected an answer."[7]

On another trip to the North, Harriet met a frightened young mulatto woman named Tilly along the Chesapeake Bay's southern shore. She had been hiding for several days with friends, anxiously waiting for Moses to come and lead her out of "Egypt." Tilly explained that she had run away because, in spite of her engagement to a man from a different plantation, her master was going to force her to marry one of his own slaves. Harriet was in a position to provide for her, so she invited Tilly to join the group.

When they got to a certain boat that Harriet had planned to take, they learned that the craft had been disabled. Instead, they were directed to a different one. Harriet only had a note from a mutual friend to the first boat's clerk instructing him to take her and her friends to the end of his route. As she walked toward the replacement boat, Harriet saw a gang of white men, who started to heckle her with racial slurs. She resolutely led the way, however, with Tilly clinging to her in terror. The clerk didn't give Harriet a ticket, though, because she didn't have the kind of pass that blacks usually carried saying they either were on their master's business or free. Instead, he instructed her to step aside until he had time to deal with her. The situation did not look at all promising.

Harriet took Tilly to the bow of the boat with her. Kneeling on a seat, she put her head on her hands and began to pray the prayer she loved, one that always reminded her Who was taking care of her: "Oh, Lord! You've been with me in six troubles, don't desert me in the seventh!" Tilly started pleading with her to see

---

[7]Ibid., 57.

about getting tickets, but Harriet kept praying the same request. Finally, the young woman spotted the clerk coming toward them. "Oh, Moses!" she cried. "The man is coming. What shall we do!" Harriet repeated her earnest plea to God until the clerk touched her shoulder. "You can come now and get your tickets," he said.

What had changed the man's entire disposition toward her? "The Lord," explained Harriet. She said that she never questioned the way the Lord chose to do a thing, just that she expected Him to act on her behalf. Like Daniel, who risked the lion's den, Harriet was prepared to accept God's will, no matter what. "Just so long as he wanted to use me, he would take care of me," she said, "and when he didn't want me no longer, I was ready to go. I always told him, 'I'm going to hold steady on to you, and you've got to see me through.'"[8]

---

[8]Ibid., 61.

8

The Lord Provides

Harriet's work was so treacherous she didn't dare make a trip into enemy territory without relying profoundly on the Lord's strength and guidance. Otherwise, she knew she didn't stand a chance against the immoral system she continually challenged.

Often God helped her in simple ways—with a new pair of shoes from Thomas Garrett, for example, or just the right amount of money to finance a rescue at just the right time. There were, however, even more dramatic instances of His work in her life; namely, those times when He gave her strong premonitions that usually foretold impending danger.

On one occasion she had the strong impression that three of her brothers were in peril. Assuming that they were probably going to be sold to a chain gang, Harriet went into action. She immediately got a friend to write a letter for her to a free black who lived near the plantation where her brothers worked. It couldn't be a straightforward letter, though, because Jacob Jackson was closely watched by community leaders who suspected him of helping slaves escape. Instead of revealing his clandestine activities, though, Jackson simply took extra precautions.

The letter Harriet dictated mostly contained pieces of "nothing" news, but its conclusion concealed a cryptic message that only Jackson would understand: "Read my letter to the old folks, and give my love to them, and tell my brothers to be always watching unto prayer, and when the good old ship of Zion comes along, to be ready to step on board."[1] Harriet asked her friend to sign the letter from William Henry Jackson, Jacob's adopted son who lived in the North. She believed that Jacob would understand that she was on her way to rescue her brothers.

Because Jackson was under suspicion, the authorities carefully examined the letters he received before passing them on to him. They couldn't understand this particular one, but the censors definitely smelled trouble. They summoned Jackson before an impromptu village tribunal and demanded that he interpret the letter for them. As his eyes scanned it quickly, the black man immediately recognized Harriet Tubman's handiwork. Reading between her lines, he realized that she wanted him to prepare her brothers for their escape from bondage. The message made sense to Jackson because he had recently heard the rumors about her brothers' imminent sale. It was to take place on the day after Christmas. How Harriet had gotten word of it, however, was beyond him.

Facing his inquisitors, Jackson pretended to read the letter extra slowly, then he put it down with a scratch of his head. "That letter can't be meant for me no how," he told them. "I can't make head or tail of it."[2]

---

[1]Bradford, 62.
[2]Ibid., 63–64.

He secretly sprang into action, though, alerting Harriet's brothers that they were about to go free.

Harriet arrived on a chilly Christmas Eve and sent word to her siblings through a messenger that she would be waiting for them at the fodder house near their parents' cabin the following night. Harriet yearned to bring out her mother and father as well, but decided to come back for them later. While her brothers were in their physical prime and about to be sold for a good price, Old Rit and Ben Ross were, at this point, too old and of too little value to be sold. They could afford to wait awhile longer.

On Christmas night Harriet was surprised when only two of the three brothers rendezvoused with her at the appointed place. None of them knew at the time that their brother John's wife had gone into labor and that John was busy getting a midwife for her. His plan was to leave as soon as the baby was born.

John's wife suspected that he was planning to run away, and, after the delivery, she confronted him. "Oh, John! You're going to leave me!" she cried. "I know it!" Although she was sobbing, she didn't beg him to stay. What good would that do when he was about to be sold away from her anyway? At least they'd have a chance to be together again someday if he escaped. "Wherever you go, John," she told him, "don't forget me and the little children."[3] He promised that as soon as possible he would return for her, and, if he couldn't go, he would send Moses.

There were other heartbreaking moments for the Ross family that Christmas. From the fodder house Harriet could see her parents moving about their cabin. Her mother looked puzzled as she kept going

---

[3] Ibid., 66.

outside, looking for her sons and their families. Why hadn't they shown up for Christmas dinner? It was going to be their last one together, maybe forever. What could have possibly kept them away? Harriet longed to race into her mother's arms and comfort her, to tell her that everything was going to be all right, but she didn't dare. Because Old Rit was high-strung, she might give Harriet away if she saw her.

To be that close and still unable to be with her mother was agonizing. Even so, Harriet did send her messenger to the cabin to tell Ben she was there. Her father hurried out to the fodder house to spend a few precious moments with his daughter, whom he hadn't seen in six years, as well as his sons. He never looked at them, though. Ben was a man of integrity, and he wanted to be able to tell Dr. Thompson truthfully after they left that, no, he hadn't seen his sons or his daughter. Without raising Old Rit's suspicions, Ben quietly returned to the cabin for some food to give his children. She never missed it.

It rained all that Christmas night as Harriet and her two brothers rested for their journey among the corn and discussed what might have happened to John. Then, just before daybreak when they couldn't wait for him any longer, he finally arrived, breathless from his ordeal. He quickly brought them up to date, and after they congratulated him on the birth of his baby, they set off. As they passed by the Ross cabin, quietly murmuring their good-byes to their parents, Old Ben came out. He had been waiting for them and had tied a handkerchief around his eyes so he couldn't actually see them. He went out with them as far as he dared, then bid them a tearful farewell. When he could no longer hear their footsteps, he took the blindfold off and quickly walked home. Sure enough, Dr.

Thompson questioned Old Ben about his sons' escape, and just as surely he answered, "I haven't seen one of them this Christmas."[4]

During a different rescue, Harriet had another of her premonitions. It was early in the spring, and she was leading her party by a river that seethed from the winter thaw and seasonal rains. Just then Harriet's heart started to pound, which was one of the ways she instinctively knew that some danger was at bay. She told the runaways that they would have to get off of the riverbank and go into the water. They stood there gaping at her in disbelief. With no time to argue or convince, Harriet moved into the frigid water, feeling it hit her body like a wall of moving ice. Not knowing what else to do, the fugitives braced themselves for impact and dutifully followed her. What happened next was like a scene straight from the life of the biblical Moses. "The water never came above my chin," Harriet recalled. "When we thought surely we were all going under, it became shallower and shallower, and we came out safe on the other side."[5] Later on, she learned that just ahead of them on the path they had been traveling, a poster had gone up with information about her and her runaways. What was worse, officers were waiting for them there, having likely heard through informers that Harriet and her group were on the way.

Although she successfully led the people through the turbulent water, Harriet paid for it later. The weather had been damp and cold that day, and she had traveled a long distance afterward in her wet clothes. She came down with a heavy cold and also developed a terrible toothache. Harriet told the story of God's rescue to Sarah Bradford on several occasions, but she never mentioned the part about getting sick. What she chose to remember about the incident was how beautifully God had protected her and the runaways. Bradford only found out about Harriet's illness through a letter Thomas Garrett wrote to her. In it he mentioned that by the time Harriet arrived at his place in Wilmington after fording that river, she was so hoarse that she could barely speak and was in considerable pain from her toothache.

In June 1857, Harriet had another premonition, this time about her parents. It was rare for aged slaves to attempt an escape because such rescues were brutal on older bodies and exhausting to their spirits. Opportunities for capture were also far greater. In fact, Harriet's close friend Franklin Sanborn said that the rescue of her parents was her "most venturous journey" just because of the risks involved.[6] Sanborn added, "Harriet carried them off with an audaciousness and an aplomb that represented complete mastery of the Railroad and perfect scorn of the white patrol. Her performance was that, at once, of the accomplished artist and the daring revolutionary."[7]

Upon arriving at Dr. Thompson's plantation, Harriet discovered that she had come in the nick of time; Ben Ross was to be tried the following Monday for his role in assisting runaways. Who knew what they might have done to him if he had been found guilty. The Lord had other plans, though. Of that time Harriet said, "I just removed my father's trial to a higher court, and brought him off to Canada."[8]

[6]Conrad, 97.
[7]Ibid., 96.
[8]Bradford, 82–83.

Ben and Old Rit were nearly seventy at the time of their escape, two of very few elderly slaves who ever made it successfully to Canada. Because the Rosses could not travel far or for very long on foot, Harriet needed a wagon in which to take them away, but how to get one? She ended up using one of Dr. Thompson's antiquated ones, as well as an old nag that he kept around the place. She doubted that he would miss them. Harriet outfitted the ancient horse with a beat-up straw collar, then put a board on the axle for her folks to sit on. She fastened another plank with ropes to the axle for a crude footrest. When she told the story to Sarah Bradford, her biographer wondered whether it had bothered Harriet's conscience to steal from her old master. Bradford concluded, "They [the slaves] had a creed of their own, and a code of morals which we dare not criticize till we find our own lives and those of our dear ones similarly imperiled."[9] Whenever possible, Harriet returned items to their owners.

Harriet drove her parents in that preposterous vehicle to the train station, where they got on board for the long journey north. When they arrived in Philadelphia, she took them to meet her friend William Still, who dutifully wrote down their stories for his records.

Old Rit and Ben told him that at the time they left, Dr. Thompson owned about twenty slaves, down from a previously much higher number. He had sold most of them because he had purchased at least twelve other farms and gotten in way over his head financially. Ben described Thompson to Still as "a rough man towards his slaves" and that although he was a Methodist minister, he had only been "pretending to

---

[9]Ibid., 72.

preach for twenty years."[10] The Rosses were still upset with him for selling two of their daughters to a chain gang years earlier, a matter that they "referred to with great feeling."[11] Harriet's parents said Thompson hadn't been a faithful shepherd of the Lord so much as "a wolf in sheep's clothing."[12]

Although Harriet received a good deal of praise from her friends and supporters because she had rescued her parents, not everyone was applauding. A proslavery propagandist named John Bell Robinson thought it was dreadful that she had taken from their home two elderly people who traveled only with difficulty. He heard Harriet speak about their escape in Boston at a women's suffrage convention in 1860. Afterward he wrote:

> The most noted point in this act of horror was the bringing away from ease and comfortable homes two old slaves over seventy years of age. Now there are no old people of any color more caressed and better taken care of than the old worn-out slaves of the south, except the wealthy whites, who are few in number. . . . This ignorant woman must have been persuaded and bewildered by flattery by some fiendish source, or she certainly would not have been guilty of such a diabolical act of wickedness and cruelty to her parents, who had a fortune laid up for old age. . . . [The women suffragists at the convention] worshiped the goddess of liberty in the shape of a poor deluded negro woman. And sing and shout with the loudest acclamations of glory and honor to her for the performance of as cruel an act as ever was performed

---

[10]Still, 395.
[11]Ibid., 396.
[12]Ibid.

by a child towards parents.[13]

Harriet understood, however, how the Evil One had deceived slavery's supporters into believing that the system was, in fact, a good one that benefited blacks. Of course, she knew the truth, and she kept trusting the Lord to guide her work in both mundane and miraculous ways.

Once while Harriet was working at a Philadelphia hotel to finance yet another journey into Maryland, she learned that the play *Uncle Tom's Cabin* had come to town. Because she was "Moses" and could relate so closely to the story, the African-Americans with whom she worked raved about the show and told her that she just had to see it. She refused, however. "I haven't got the heart to go and see the sufferings of my people played upon the stage," she said. "I've heard 'Uncle Tom's Cabin' read, and I tell you Mrs. Stowe's pen hasn't begun to paint what slavery is at the far South. I've seen the real thing, and I don't want to see it on any stage or in any theatre."[14]

---

[13]Conrad, 99–100.
[14]Conrad, 56.

9

Harriet the Activist

Harriet Tubman didn't spend all of her time rescuing slaves during the 1850s, but she was constantly thinking about it, always planning for her next journey. Even her friendships revolved around abolitionism; most of her confidants, both blacks and whites, were active participants in the Underground Railroad.

One of the most powerful abolitionists, William H. Seward, served as New York's governor, then was one of its two senators, and he went on to become Abraham Lincoln's secretary of state. An ardent foe of slavery, Seward was among Harriet's closest friends. In 1857 he sold his home in Auburn, New York, to her so that Ben and Old Rit wouldn't have to suffer through another brutally cold Canadian winter. The small frame house at the end of South Street became a refuge for them and for Harriet from the battles she fought constantly to destroy slavery.

The temptation to settle down in one's home—away from the turmoil of saving fugitives—might have enticed a person less resolute than Harriet. If not that, perhaps the knowledge that between forty thousand dollars and sixty thousand dollars had been offered by slave owners to anyone who might capture the infamous "Moses."

In Maryland, the authorities were looking for Harriet aggressively, and slaveholders boasted about the torture they would gladly inflict if they ever got their hands on her. In light of the extraordinary dangers, some of Harriet's friends tried to convince her not to return for more slaves. Surely she had done enough for "the cause," they said. She would not be dissuaded, though. The Lord still had work for her to do, and He would protect her while she was engaged in it. Even if He did choose to let her die, she would have proved faithful to His purpose. All that, and heaven, too. It was, for Harriet, a win-win situation, not a desperate one.

In the late 1850s, Harriet became part of the Boston lecture circuit, compelled by her need to pay for the house she had purchased from Mr. and Mrs. Seward. Although Harriet had been attending anti-slavery events for some years, she didn't become a speaker until 1858. Still, her presence had been memorable. Historian William Wells recalled:

> For eight or ten years previous to the breaking out of the Rebellion, all who frequented anti-slavery conventions, lectures, picnics, and fairs, could not fail to have seen a black woman of medium size, upper front teeth gone, smiling countenance, attired in coarse, but neat apparel, with an old-fashioned reticule or bag suspended by her side, and who, on taking her seat, would at once drop off into a sound sleep.[1]

Once Harriet began to speak at abolitionist gath-

---

[1]Conrad, 71.

erings, she proved to be a powerful and eloquent speaker who mesmerized her audiences with stranger-than-fiction tales of nail-biting rescues. Abolitionists enjoyed giving the platform to former slaves such as Harriet because they could speak more convincingly than whites—or always-free blacks—about the evils of captivity. There were risks involved for the speakers, however. Sometimes pro-slavery agitators showed up, and they could get violent. One of them broke Frederick Douglass's wrist at an outdoor meeting in Indiana.

There was another danger for Harriet. She had to protect her identity when she spoke publicly because she never knew when an informer might be in an audience waiting to capture her for some fabulous reward money. In those days before television, or even the widespread use of photography, it was not difficult to conceal one's identity. During Harriet's speaking engagements in Boston, her minister-friend Thomas Wentworth Higginson introduced her as "Moses." It wasn't only as a show of respect. He used the nickname because Harriet was a much-wanted woman who needed to be protected.

She was sometimes introduced by other names, as well. For example, when she spoke at the New England Colored Citizens' Convention, the host presented her as "Miss Harriet Garrison." This was an obvious tribute to one of the greatest abolitionists, William Lloyd Garrison, publisher of the movement's most respected and widely circulated newspaper, *The Liberator*. It is, however, the only recorded case of Harriet's use of that particular alias.

Because of her new prominence, Harriet became an intimate associate of New England's literary elite, having been introduced to many writers by her friends

Thomas Higginson and Franklin Sanborn. Harriet
was a guest in the homes of Lydia Marie Child, Amos
Bronson Alcott, the father of Louisa May Alcott, Mrs.
Horace Mann, and Ralph Waldo Emerson. Although
these white men and women of high breeding and education came from a different world than Harriet,
they deeply admired and respected her. She, in turn,
felt at ease with them.

> In her ringing discourse, in her assured bear-
> ing of equality with all others, the anti-slavery
> leaders saw justified all for which they fought,
> saw the black people in freedom and in flour-
> ish. . . . Harriet had long since discovered that
> there were white people with fine souls, and she
> had learned to give hers to these. As a child en-
> slaved, she had always dreamed of kind, white
> women, and here, in Abolition, she had found
> them.[2]

The Reverend Higginson, who came from Worces-
ter, Massachusetts, became one of Harriet's most fervent admirers. He regarded her more highly than any
other woman of that time. In June 1859, he wrote
glowingly—though inaccurately on some points—of
her to his mother:

> We have had the greatest heroine of the age
> here, Harriet Tubman, a black woman, and a fu-
> gitive slave, who has been back eight times se-
> cretly and brought out in all sixty slaves with her,
> including all her own family, besides aiding many
> more in other ways to escape. Her tales of adven-
> ture are beyond anything in fiction and her inge-
> nuity and generalship are extraordinary. I have

---

[2]Ibid., 141.

known her for some time and mentioned her in speeches once or twice—the slaves call her Moses. She has had a reward of twelve thousand dollars offered for her in Maryland and will probably be burned alive whenever she is caught, which she probably will be, first or last, as she is going again.[3]

On July 4, 1859, Higginson escorted Harriet to Framingham for a special event for friends and members of the Massachusetts Anti-Slavery Society. The speech she delivered there was powerful. She described the slaves' terrible plight and her rescues so vividly that the Society's secretary became mesmerized and couldn't write down her message for posterity. When it was over, he finally scribbled, "Mere words could do no justice to the speaker, and therefore we do not undertake to give them; but we advise all our readers to take the earliest opportunity to see and hear her."[4]

In addition to her appearances at abolitionist meetings, Harriet spoke at women's suffrage conferences. The two causes were closely linked in antebellum America, both receiving their moral stimulus from Christianity. Harriet became well acquainted with Elizabeth Cady Stanton, Lucretia Mott, and Susan B. Anthony, who assisted her work financially and materially. Everywhere Harriet appeared audiences found her a compelling speaker who not only wowed them with her stories, but who also challenged them to act. All this while sometimes suffering from sleeping spells right on the platform. She was, per-

---

[3]Ibid., 107.
[4]Ibid., 109.

haps, the only speaker in American history who ever put herself to sleep.

While Harriet earned some money as a speaker to pay for her home, support her parents, and continue her rescue work in Maryland, she also expected the Lord to use her friends and her connections to provide some of the supplies and equipment. As in all other matters in her life, she took seriously the promise that God would supply all her needs according to His riches in glory in Christ Jesus. After discerning a need, she would go to the Lord and ask Him to send someone who could fill it.

Harriet's friends seemed only too happy to be part of this "divine pipeline," although at times it frustrated them that she was constantly taking care of others, while paying little or no attention to her own needs. She wouldn't hesitate to ask her friends for material or financial assistance for her work, but Harriet wouldn't request anything that was only for herself. One day she asked William Seward for emergency assistance, and he uncharacteristically complained about it. "Harriet, you have worked for others long enough," he told her. "If you would ever ask anything for yourself, I would gladly give it to you, but I will not help you to rob yourself for others any longer."[5]

If the Lord told her that someone had money for her, Harriet would wait stubbornly until it came. An example of this is the time she had decided to return to Maryland for her parents. Harriet sensed that the Lord wanted her to seek financial assistance from a friend in New York City. She told the people with whom she was staying at the time, "I'm going to [his] office, and I ain't going to leave there, and I ain't going

---

[5]Bradford, 89.

to eat or drink, till I get money enough to take me down after the old people."

When Harriet's friend invited her into his office and asked after her health, she was both blunt and to the point. "I want some money, sir."

"You do!" he said, surprised by her boldness. "How much do you want?"

"I want twenty dollars, sir," came the response.

"Twenty dollars! Who told you to come here for twenty dollars!"

Without hesitation Harriet replied, "The Lord told me, sir."

Although it would be difficult to argue with that, this man did because he simply didn't have that kind of money. "Well, I guess the Lord's mistaken this time," he said.

Harriet wouldn't budge. "No, sir," she insisted. "The Lord's never been mistaken! Anyhow, I'm going to sit here till I get it."

And sit she did. The warmth of the office, combined with her lack of activity, brought one of her sleeps on Harriet, but then she woke up and talked with people coming in and out of her friend's busy office. This went on throughout the afternoon as she alternately watched people come and go and dozed off. Harriet's friend implored her to leave, begging her to realize that he didn't have twenty dollars, but she refused to leave without it. After all, *the Lord* had told her to go there for help. Word of what was happening there got out during the day. By the time Harriet awakened from her final sleep of that long day, her friend presented her with a total of sixty dollars that people had collected and left for her.[6]

---

[6]Ibid., 81–82.

On another occasion, Harriet went to see Thomas Garrett for help, which was her usual custom when passing through Wilmington. He always furnished her with what she needed to whatever extent he was able, especially with shoes from his store. The generous Quaker was happy that his friend had returned to him.

"Harriet, I am glad to see thee! I suppose thee wants a pair of new shoes." But he was mistaken.

"Well, not exactly," she told him. "I want more than that."

Garrett thought he would tease her. "I have always been liberal with thee, and wish to be; but I am not rich, and cannot afford to give much."

Harriet persisted. "God tells me you have money for me," she said.

Garrett did have some cash that he had collected waiting for her, but he wanted to have some fun with her first about her simple, staunch conviction that God had spoken to her yet again. Perhaps God had deceived her this time, he suggested. She wouldn't even consider that possibility, though. If God had told her that Garrett had money for her, then Garrett had money for her, and it was twenty-three dollars she happened to be needing.

Garrett later recalled, "I then gave her twenty-four dollars and some odd cents, the net proceeds of five pounds sterling, received through Eliza Wigham, of Scotland, for her."[7]

Wigham headed up an anti-slavery society where Garrett had spoken while visiting Scotland. He had described the abolitionist activities with which he was involved, and some people were so moved that after-

---

[7] Ibid., 86.

ward they asked how they might help his friend Harriet Tubman. Through that connection, he became a channel for an informal funding network.

Some time later, Harriet went to see Garrett with the same message; God had told her that the Quaker had money for her, "but not so much as before." Indeed, a few days earlier he had received "one pound, ten shillings" from his Scottish friends for her work.

Although Harriet's friends supported her work, they did sometimes try to pull in the reins a bit, fearing for her welfare. Tensions over slavery had heightened to a frenzied level in Maryland in the waning years of the 1850s, and Harriet was at the center of the fire storm. The Reverend Thomas Higginson was especially concerned and solemnly warned her that if she went down there again, she would "certainly be caught and burned alive."[8] Harriet never wavered, however, in her resolve to end slavery no matter the cost to her personally. On one occasion, though, she didn't even have to leave New York State to rescue a slave.

On April 27, 1860, Harriet was on her way to a big anti-slavery gathering in Boston at the invitation of her friend Congressman Gerrit Smith. While at the train station in Troy, New York, she noticed a surging crowd near the courthouse and stopped to find out what was going on. Harriet discovered that a runaway named Charles Nalle had been apprehended and was to be tried. The tall, handsome man was around thirty and had been his half-brother's slave in Culpepper County, Virginia. The light-skinned Nalle had fled north and found employment in Troy as a coachman for Mr. Uri Gilbert. A newspaperman who was ac-

---

[8]Conrad, 105.

quainted with Nalle's owner tipped him off regarding the slave's whereabouts.

Around eleven o'clock that morning Nalle was on his way to purchase bread when U.S. Marshal J. W. Holmes arrested him at the bakery and took him to U.S. Commissioner Miles Beach. Harriet instantly became involved. She pushed her way into the building where Nalle was being held. There was so much agitation in the street below that the police fretted about bringing Nalle downstairs from the commissioner's second floor office. People stood nose-to-nose arguing that he should go free, while others insisted, "The law must be obeyed!" A group of anti-slavery people shouted up to the window that they would buy Nalle. The offers went from twelve hundred dollars to fifteen hundred dollars.

Harriet quickly assessed the situation, her years of covert activity in Maryland helping her know what needed to be done and how. She sprang to action, grabbing a little boy by the collar. "Go into the street," she said, "and yell 'Fire!' " When he did, at the top of his lungs, the ringing of bells suddenly filled the air, and the crowd increased.

Harriet whipped out her sunbonnet as part of her plan to masquerade as an old woman. Then she stooped her shoulders and went up to the commissioner's office, where one policeman tried to get her out of harm's way. "Come, old woman, you must get out of this," he said. "I must have the way cleared. If you can't get down alone, someone will help you."[9]

Finally, a path was opened for Nalle to go through. The frightened man emerged from the building with his wrists handcuffed, walking between the U.S. mar-

[9]Bradford, 121.

shal and another officer. Behind them followed his master. "Here he comes!" Harriet suddenly yelled from an upstairs window. "Take him!"[10] Then she rushed down the stairs and instructed some bystanders to hustle Nalle down to the river. She knocked down several men who were trying to get to him, and in the excitement, Nalle eluded them. When she reached his side a few minutes later, Harriet shoved a policeman who was trying to arrest him as she kept yelling, "Don't let them take him!" She got roughed up a bit, too. Her coat was torn, and her shoes pulled right off from her feet, but Harriet wouldn't stop trying to help Nalle. It was her duty to go to the aid of any runaway.

She managed to transfer her bonnet to Nalle's head so that he might be mistaken in the surging crowd for an old woman. Then Harriet waved to a man with a horse and wagon to hand it over. Nalle endured a tense boat ride across the river, where the authorities once again seized him. They took him to the third story of a house. Some children in the street told Harriet where he was when she arrived in a separate ferryboat from the one Nalle had used. She hurried into the house and saw on the stairs the bodies of two men who had been shot in the melee. Using her great physical strength, Harriet picked Nalle up and carried him downstairs where a man drove him off with a horse and wagon. Nalle successfully escaped to Schenectady, and eventually settled a bit farther west. Harriet hid for two days on the outskirts of Troy until the furor blew over.

---

[10]Ibid., 122.

She was ready to do anything at any time and any place to free a slave. It is little wonder, then, that she joined forces with the nation's most famous—or infamous—abolitionist.

10

"General" Tubman Meets John Brown

Among abolitionists in the 1850s, Harriet Tubman was one of the most venerated *and* the most despised. There was another, however, whose very name still rouses passion among people today—John Brown. As a young man, he vowed to spend his life removing the stain of slavery from the nation's fabric, no matter what it involved for him personally. Slavery was so abhorrent to him that he deemed any measures to abolish it justifiable. There was no moral ambiguity in him, no margin for compromise.

Brown and his five sons burst onto the national scene in mid-decade when a civil war broke out in Kansas. In it they took part in the murder of five men, four of whom were hacked to death. The event came to be known as the Pottawatomi massacre, and Brown gained an understandable reputation for vicious fanaticism. The event that sparked the war occurred in 1854, when the Missouri Compromise, which banned slavery north of the Mason-Dixon Line, was invali-

dated by the Kansas-Nebraska Act. The latter allowed
Kansans to decide for themselves whether their territory would be slave or free. Although most of the earlier pioneers to that area were peace-loving and didn't
want any part of the volatile slavery issue, a hoard of
settlers on both sides of the conflict flooded the prairie
state to make sure it would go in their direction. That
was concurrent with a March 1855 election for the ter-
ritorial legislature in which both factions strived for
majority representation.

John Brown was considered an extremist by many
people of his time. Nevertheless, he inspired fervent
loyalty among his advocates because his cause was itself so just. Peaceful, even-tempered Harriet Tubman
was one of his most devoted admirers because he, a
white man, was risking everything to secure her people's freedom. One may wonder, however, how she
could agree with Brown's violent methods. Earl Conrad offered a possible explanation: "She gave sanction
and association to conspiracy and insurrection when
she believed that these methods were necessary to the
freedom of her people."[1]

To abolish slavery, Harriet favored any technique
that would get the job done, from legislation to moral
persuasion, from education to insurrection. Even a
large-scale military struggle would be justified, she
believed, if that's what it took to eliminate slavery.[2]

Harriet's views, along with Brown's, matched the
prevailing motivation behind the abolitionist movement of the 1850s in which "the need for black and
white collaboration in the face of a common enemy, the
resources of the Underground Railroad, insurrection-

---

[1]Conrad, 127.
[2]Blockson, *The Underground Railroad*, 142.

ary theory (especially the experience of previous American revolts), and Christian zeal or the moral right of the Negro to freedom" were crucial.[3] Abolitionists likened Harriet's mission to rescue slaves to a war—"a raid upon an entrenched and an armed army."[4]

The two celebrated abolitionists met for the first time in early April 1858 while Harriet was concluding another winter in St. Catherines, Ontario. The black pastor J. W. Loguen of Syracuse, New York, accompanied Brown to Canada after Congressman Gerrit Smith strongly encouraged him to get to know Harriet. Along the way, Frederick Douglass received Brown and reiterated what Smith had said, that Harriet might be valuable to him in an operation that Brown was formulating to overthrow slavery. When the two finally met, Harriet made a potent impression on Brown. "The first I see is General Tubman, the second is General Tubman, and the third is General Tubman," he remarked. From him, it was a high compliment, and ever after he referred to Harriet as "General."

Brown believed that Harriet's knowledge of Underground Railroad routes could be very important to him. Those operating in Virginia, Maryland, and Pennsylvania were especially critical. He was counting on the assistance of various "station masters" there to provide him with manpower and supplies for his mission. In addition, he asked Harriet if she would recruit men from among the slaves she had rescued who were now living in Canada. She was only too happy to help him plan his campaign. In addition to

---

[3]Ibid., 113–14.
[4]Ibid., 42.

obtaining volunteers for Brown, she also told him what routes she used in Maryland, and drew simple maps of them for him to use.

Harriet had a gift for discerning who was her friend and who should be avoided. In this case, she instinctively trusted John Brown.

Over the years she had had a recurring dream, and a particularly vexing one at that. In it she found herself in a wilderness setting when she suddenly spotted a serpent. Then its head was transformed into that of a white-bearded old man. As if that wasn't startling enough, two younger heads rose up beside his. Unexpectedly a great crowd rushed in and struck down the younger heads while the older one continued to gaze wistfully at Harriet.

When Harriet first set eyes upon John Brown, she realized with a start that the man in the dream was "the very image of the head she had seen."[5] Although she still didn't understand the meaning of the bizarre dream, it seemed to her that God had sent it to prepare her for an alliance with this passionate supporter of her people.

Brown came away from that first meeting in April 1858 with Harriet's pledge that when the time came for his campaign to free large numbers of slaves, she would personally bring her following of free men to him from Canada. He also asked if she would be willing to guide the newly freed slaves back up north. She readily agreed. It promised to be one of her most dangerous rescues, but Harriet was ready to embark on this daring crusade for the sake of her persecuted people.

The following month, Harriet assumed a pivotal

[5]Bradford, 118.

role at a Chatham, Ontario, convention to draw up a plan for the abolitionist government Brown hoped to carve out in the state of Virginia. Also in attendance were a few dozen people whom Harriet had brought out of Maryland and whom she had enlisted for Brown's operation. John Brown was thrilled with her efforts. To one of his sons he wrote effusively of Harriet's physical prowess, showing how deeply she had impressed him. "Harriet Tubman hooked on her whole team [of horses] at once," he said. "[Harriet] is the most of a man naturally that I ever met with. There is abundant material here and of the right quality."[6]

What exactly did John Brown have in mind for his slave-freeing invasion? He wanted to form an abolitionist republic in the Appalachian Mountains and from there carry out a guerilla war against slavery using sympathetic whites and fugitive slaves in his army. He prepared for this by studying successful slave uprisings that had taken place earlier in Brazil and Jamaica. Harriet became an integral part of this strategy because of her knowledge, experience, and convictions. She took her role in creating his overall strategy with the utmost gravity, meeting several times with Brown to plan the onslaught. Harriet encouraged Brown to begin his remarkable operation on the historically symbolic date of July 4. When Harriet and Brown couldn't be together in person, they used Frederick Douglass as an intermediary to convey messages to each other.

Harriet was in the best position to help Brown that spring of 1858, but his plans suddenly went awry when a man named Hugh Forbes, a mercenary type who had hooked up with him, betrayed Brown's

---

[6]Ibid., 96.

scheme to Senator Hugh Wilson. The campaign had to be postponed, and critical momentum was lost as a result. By the time Brown would act, Harriet would not be in a position to help him.

During the winter that followed, they met in Boston, where Harriet was on her first speaking tour, trying to raise funds to pay for her house and her continuing slave rescues. She also hoped to recruit more free blacks in Boston for her friend's crusade. The strain of all this activity proved too much, however, even for someone as physically strong as Harriet was. Nearing collapse, she convalesced at a friend's house in New Bedford, Massachusetts, remaining there for several months.

Things in general were not going the way Brown had anticipated. For example, when he decided that it would be best to have a leading African-American by his side at the time of the operation and asked Frederick Douglass to fill the role, the orator turned him down. Douglass simply didn't believe that from a military standpoint the plan would succeed at that time. Rather than heed the black elder statesman's advice, however, Brown decided to go with Harriet Tubman instead. The only problem was that he didn't know where she was.

Time was wasting, and because Brown feared treason and was facing many other obstacles, he decided to go ahead with the battle. He first showed up in the vicinity of the Potomac River around the Fourth of July, the date Harriet had suggested, only a year later than she had hoped. Earlier that spring, Brown had rented a barn under the name "Isaac Smith" and used it to store guns, ammunition, and supplies. Not having heard to the contrary, he assumed Harriet was still at work assembling a large group of free black volunteers.

In mid-September Lewis Hayden, an African-American abolitionist from Boston, discovered that Harriet was recovering from her illness in New Bedford, and he sent an urgent message to her. "You must come to Boston at once," he said. Harriet was alarmed because she had been out of commission for so long and was, by now, way behind in her efforts to recruit soldiers for Brown's freedom army. She started out for Virginia, but when she got as far as New York, she learned that she was too late.

On the night of October 16, 1859, Brown, five blacks, and thirteen whites seized the federal arsenal at Harpers Ferry, Virginia. During the affair they killed the mayor and took some of the town's other leaders as prisoners. Two days later the state militia, led by Colonel Robert E. Lee, closed in, and only five of Brown's conspirators escaped. One of his sons died in the conflict, and a second one went to the gallows.

Still in New York with friends on October 17, Harriet's heart suddenly started to flutter, then it pounded hard, as it so often did when she had a premonition. As she later learned, at that very time John Brown had been taken prisoner at Harpers Ferry. Of Harriet's failure to assist Brown when he needed her, the black intellectual W. E. B. Dubois once said, "Only sickness, brought on by her toil and exposure, prevented Harriet from being present at Harpers Ferry."[7]

Bells tolled throughout the free states when Brown was hanged on December 2, content "to die for God's eternal truth." At last, Harriet knew the meaning of her persistent dream about him; the great man's sons

---

[7]Conrad, 126.

had died, and the head, Brown himself, was forsaken.

Harriet decided it was best to drop out of sight for a while because her name was mentioned in the Senate committee investigating the touchy incident that led the nation that much closer to war. It wasn't until much later, however, that the full extent of her involvement with Brown and his campaign was known publicly.[8]

Some time later, while she was visiting Franklin Sanborn at his home, Harriet saw a bust of John Brown in a place of honor. "The sight of it, which was new to her, threw her into a sort of ecstasy of sorrow and admiration," he said, "and she went on in her own rhapsodical way to pronounce his apotheosis."[9] As she stood there gazing at the bust, Harriet told Sanborn, "It was not John Brown that died at Charleston. It was Christ—the savior of our people."[10] Perhaps Harriet was thinking of the tribute paid to Brown by her friend Ralph Waldo Emerson:

> That new saint, than whom nothing purer or more brave was ever led by love of men into conflict and death . . . will make the gallows glorious like the cross.[11]

Because Harriet regarded Brown as a courageous man of God and a true liberator of her people, she never stopped singing his praises. In fact, she thought more highly of him than of the man who eventually did liberate the slaves—Abraham Lincoln. In the early part of Lincoln's presidency, Harriet thought he

---

[8]Ibid., 128.

[9]Ibid., 143.

[10]Ibid.

[11]Samuel Eliot Morison, *The Oxford History of the American People* (New York: Oxford University Press, 1965), 602.

vacillated about emancipation. There had been no shadow of turning with John Brown, however.

After her friend's death, Harriet became restless. She had a strong feeling that war between the states was now inevitable. According to an article written about her during that time, "she took refuge from her perplexity in the mysteries of her fervid religion."[12] She also continued to rescue family members and other slaves who yearned for freedom.

Harriet's last trip to Maryland came near the end of 1860 and continued into the new year, the one in which the war would begin. At that time, she brought out a family of five, consisting of Stephen and Maria Ennets and their three children: Harriet, who was six, Amanda, four, and a three-month-old baby. They arrived at Thomas Garrett's place in Wilmington on November 30, where they were joined by a Baltimore woman who was expecting a baby and wanted to go on with them to Canada. The old Quaker gave Harriet ten dollars to hire a man and a carriage to get them across the river to Chester County, Pennsylvania, but he took Harriet aside and told her that he was gravely concerned for her safety. There were increased patrols on the roads, he said, and ruthless slave catchers were more eager than ever to capture her. Nevertheless, he had confidence in her and in God. "There is now much more risk than there has been for many months," Garrett told a mutual friend, "yet as it is Harriet who seems to have a special angel to guide her on her journeys of mercy, I continue to have hope."[13]

In February, when Harriet and her runaways reached New York City, her friends there were just as

---

[12]Bradford, 118.
[13]Still, 531.

apprehensive as Garrett. They insisted that, given the explosive mood of the country, she not linger but instead leave for Canada right away. Once she made it safely across the border, Harriet stayed with her group in St. Catherines until the spring, when a new and equally trying chapter in her life, and the nation's, would commence.

11

A Nation at War

Harriet made her last trip to Maryland in the winter of 1860–61, but that wasn't the end of her mission to liberate her people. The Civil War broke out in the spring, creating new challenges and tensions for southern slaves. It also presented a new opportunity for Moses to deliver them.

In the initial months of the conflict, Massachusetts Governor John Andrew sent Harriet a letter asking if she would consider serving her people—as well as her country—in the Union army. It would require her willingness to leave at a moment's notice, he said, as soon as he could get government approval. According to his plan, Harriet would function as a nurse, spy, and scout on the South Carolina coast, where an emissary was needed between newly freed slaves and their Union liberators.

It couldn't have been an easy decision for Harriet. She was concerned about her aged parents, who were dependent upon her for their health and welfare, as well as the indigent blacks who kept streaming to her home in Auburn for assistance. She realized, however, that she was not an "island," that there were many

good-hearted people in the community, including
some of her brothers and sisters, who had looked after
those folks during her absences in the past. After only
a few moments of reflection, Harriet knew what she
needed to do. A great opportunity—a tremendous new
duty—had arisen, and she was determined to do her
best to answer that call. As she had hoped, the good
people of Auburn looked after her loved ones and the
other dependents while she was away.

It wasn't until May of the following year, however,
that the way became clear for Harriet to enter the
Union army. At that time she boarded a government
transport, *The Atlantic*, and sailed to the South Carolina Sea Islands, where she reported to Brigadier
General David Hunter. Many slaves had flocked to the
Union forces, seeking freedom from their masters and
finding work within the Union lines. Known as "contraband" in the months before emancipation, the
slaves labored in a support capacity, making meals,
digging trenches, and performing other important services for the army.

Harriet threw herself wholeheartedly into her
work, in spite of her disappointment with the com-
mander in chief of the Union effort, Abraham Lincoln.
She believed that the president's first objective for the
war should have been the emancipation of slaves
rather than preventing secession or preserving the
Union. Before leaving for South Carolina, she had told
an audience that she didn't think the North would win
the war until Lincoln got his priorities in order. In
Harriet's lively storytelling fashion she said,

> God won't let Master Lincoln beat the South
> till he does the right thing. Master Lincoln is a
> great man, and I'm a poor negro, but this negro

can tell Master Lincoln how to save money and young men. He can do it by setting the negroes free. Suppose there was an awfully big snake down there on the floor. Then he bites you. Folks get all scared because you might die. You send for a doctor to cut the bite, but the snake rolls up there, and while the doctor is doing it, it bites you again. The doctor cuts out that bite, too, but while he's doing it, the snake just springs up and bites you again, and so he keeps going until you kill the snake. That is what Master Lincoln ought to know.[1]

During the first few months Harriet spent in South Carolina, she reported to surgeon Henry Durrant at the Contraband Hospital in Beaufort and mainly nursed blacks who had fallen ill. For her work, some say Harriet received a soldier's pay, which was fifteen dollars per month; however, the story of her compensation is convoluted. According to one version, the contrabands became jealous because Harriet was drawing a paycheck for her work and they were not. They believed that the army was showing her favoritism. Because she wanted to win their support and confidence, Harriet stopped taking pay from the army and started supporting herself.[2] According to Earl Conrad, however, from the beginning of her "solicited" though "irregular attachment" with the Union army, Harriet had known that she would be responsible for her own financial support.[3]

Another version of the story says that Harriet was being compensated by the government but stopped

---

[1]Eugene Genovese, et al., *The World the Slaves Made* (New York: Vintage Books, 1972), 438.
[2]Conrad, 160.
[3]Ibid.

taking pay as a matter of principle. When free black troops came to Hilton Head under the command of Colonels Robert Shaw of Boston and James Montgomery, a bearded Kansan who had fought with John Brown in that territory, she discovered that the black soldiers were only given seven dollars, less than half of what the whites received. As a result, Harriet protested the discrimination by refusing her own pay. Since Montgomery helped put together one of the nation's initial black units, the First Regiment of South Carolina Volunteers, in January 1863, after the emancipation was announced, she would have drawn a salary for about nine months.

Sarah Bradford, to whom Harriet told her life story, said that Harriet wasn't "allowed" pay and had to support herself. Bradford commented that "this woman sacrificed everything, and left her nearest and dearest, and risked her life hundreds of times for the cause of the Union, without one cent of recompense."[4] Given her close relationship with Harriet and the intimate access she had to her, it would seem that Bradford was closest to the truth of the matter.

Harriet's precarious financial position meant putting in long nights as well as long days. Following an exhausting day of ministrations to the sick under largely primitive conditions, Harriet would return to her cabin and start baking, an activity that would continue far into the night, no matter how hot and sticky the Deep South got. She wouldn't stop until she had produced some fifty pies, a great deal of gingerbread, and two casks of root beer. The next morning she would hire one of the contrabands to sell the food and drink through the Union camps. In this completely

---

[4]Bradford, 95.

unselfish way, minus all resentment and bitterness, Harriet supported herself when most people would have told the Union army to find someone else to do its dirty work.[5]

Harriet was completely dedicated to her people. She used the money she earned, literally by the sweat of her brow, to help blacks become self-sufficient by building a community washhouse for them so they could earn money by washing the army's laundry. Not only did this contribute to their independence; it helped develop their self-respect as well.

Years later Harriet described to Sarah Bradford what it was like to work at the Contraband Hospital.

> Well, I'd go to the hospital, I would, early every morning. I'd get a big chunk of ice, I would, and put it in a basin, and fill it with water. Then I'd take a sponge and begin. The first man I'd come to, I'd thrash away the flies, and they'd rise, they would, like bees around a hive. Then I'd begin to bathe the wounds, and by the time I'd bathed off three or four, the fire and heat would have melted the ice and made the water warm, and it would be as red as clear blood. Then I'd go and get more ice, I would, and by the time I got to the next ones, the flies would be around the first ones black and thick as ever.[6]

Up and down the South Carolina coast Harriet labored in several different Union hospitals, including ones used exclusively for soldiers. It seemed there was no task too difficult for her to tackle. As far south as Florida, she delivered babies and ministered to sick and dying soldiers, who were "dying off like sheep"

---

[5]Ibid., 97.
[6]Ibid.

from dysentery.[7] In order to relieve their suffering, Harriet prepared a medicine from roots growing near the waters that had created the disease. It helped to alleviate the outbreak when all other remedies had failed the doctors. She also nursed hundreds of people who had smallpox and "malignant fevers."[8]

After rescuing slaves from Maryland and finding them enough food, clothes, and shelter while dodging the artifices of slave catchers and their dogs of prey, other hardships must have seemed more or less the same to Harriet. But there was another reason for her courage and benevolence. She wasn't afraid of death in any form. She continued to hold fast to the conviction that "the Lord will take care of me until my time comes, and then I'm ready to go."[9]

In addition to her nursing, Harriet also operated as a Union spy. She gathered information about troop movements, supply sources, populations, and artillery positions of the Confederate army. To do her espionage, Harriet often resorted to tricks she had learned while whisking slaves away from their masters, such as dressing like an old woman. She was frequently under fire. Harriet also set up a spy network among blacks on plantations, which resulted in successful raids in Georgia and Florida that she helped carry out, along with her minister-friend from New York, Colonel Thomas Wentworth Higginson, and Colonel Montgomery. For her reconnaissance missions she was given nine scouts and river pilots to work under her command. For her protection she carried roughly a dozen letters of recommendation. If anyone questioned her identity or her activities, she could produce those letters to back up her claims.[10]

Harriet's most celebrated mission as a spy and scout came in early June 1863 on the Combahee River when she led a raid that she had organized. The objective was to remove torpedoes that the Confederates had placed in the river as booby traps to destroy railroads and bridges and cut off Union supplies. Harriet undertook the treacherous mission under the condition that Colonel James Montgomery would lead the overall expedition. She had special affection and respect for him because he had served with her beloved John Brown in Kansas.

On June 2 Harriet's troops surprised two Confederate encampments and were able to free around eight hundred slaves. Trouble quickly ensued, however, when the frightened blacks refused to get on Union boats. How did they know whether they really could trust the Yankees, whom their masters had vilified continually? At the same time, they were petrified of returning to slavery. As if to underscore the point, their owners were on the scene, trying to persuade them with the whip to come back. The slaves were frozen in terror of the unknown, as well as the horrors they already were fleeing.

The scene became chaotic. In order to reassure and encourage the slaves in the midst of the discord, Harriet mounted one of the gunboats and called out in a loud voice to the frightened blacks. Everything would be all right, she said, if they would get on board the Union boats. Uncle Sam was going to take good care of them. Her reassuring and commanding presence caused them to turn away from their masters and run toward the gunboats. A new problem developed, how-

---

[10]Conrad, 179.

ever, when they clung for dear life to the vessels, which, as a result, couldn't pull away from the shore. Harriet thought that singing might soothe their agitated spirits and create a more orderly way of evacuation, so she lifted up her compelling voice and sang a tune that she made up as she went along:

> Of all the whole creation
> in the East or in the West,
> The glorious Yankee nation
> is the greatest and the best.
>
> Come along! Come along!
> Don't be alarmed,
> Uncle Sam is rich enough
> to give you all a farm.
>
> Come along! Come along!
> Don't be a fool!
> Uncle Sam's rich enough
> to send us all to school!

To Harriet's delight, it worked. At the end of each verse, the slaves threw up their hands and shouted, "Glory!" Because they no longer were clinging to the boats, the vessels were able to pull out from the shore. Harriet said she never would forget the experience.

I never saw such a sight. We laughed, and laughed, and laughed. Here you'd see a woman with a pail on her head, rice smoking in it just as she'd taken it from the fire, a young one hanging on behind, one hand around her forehead to hold on, the other hand digging into the rice-pot, eating with all its might. Holding onto her dress were two or three more. Down her back was a bag with a pig in it. One woman brought two pigs, a white one and a black one. We took them all on board and named the white pig Beauregard and the black pig Jeff Davis. Sometimes the women would come with twins hanging around their necks. It appeared like I never saw so many twins in my life. Bags on their shoulders, baskets on their heads, pigs squealing, chickens screaming, young ones squalling.[11]

The evacuation proceeded in an orderly and congenial manner until everyone was aboard and taken out of harm's way and to the Union encampment. Harriet's mission was accomplished. This was a real blow to the slaveholders, however, who had lost valuable laborers.

Although the Deep South slaves came to trust this valiant sister, Harriet admitted that at times she was vexed by their dialect and customs. She said, "Why, their language down there in the far South is just as different from ours in Maryland as you can think. They laughed when they heard me talk, and I could not understand them, nohow."[12]

One time Harriet attended one of their midnight funerals, which took place at that particular time because of an old and somewhat obscure plantation rule that slaves couldn't be buried during the day. People settled around the rude casket as pine torches illuminated the eerie scene. The black preacher had everyone sing a hymn, and he then moved into a lengthy sermon. He proclaimed in passionate tones that everyone had to die someday, and that everyone had better be ready because death was inescapable. "Who of all this congregation is going next to lie dead-ah-dead-ah?" he shouted and gestured at them. "You

[11]Bradford, 100–101.
[12]Ibid., 103.

can't go nowhere, my friends and brothers, but death will find you."[13] The rousing and repetitive message was followed by a dance called the "spiritual shuffle." In it everyone shook hands with everyone else, calling each other by name as they sang:

My sister Mary's bound to go;
My sister Nanny's bound to go;
My brother Tony's bound to go;
My brother July's bound to go.[14]

After that continued for some time, a government wagon carried the coffin to its place of burial as the mourners processed along with it.

Harriet spent two demanding years with the Military Department of the South, giving herself to her people with unselfish abandon. The physical toll was so great, however, that in the spring of 1864, exhausted and weak, her sleeping spells worsening, she returned to Auburn. This time she was the one to whom blacks and whites, as well as her parents, ministered. It was during that time of convalescence that she became close to Sarah Bradford, an abolitionist who eventually wrote the story of Harriet's extraordinary life.

By August, Harriet had recovered sufficiently enough to visit her close friends in Boston. During this time she met another African-American heroine, Sojourner Truth, who was on her way to Washington for an audience with Abraham Lincoln.

As Harriet reflected years later on her own opportunities to meet the president while serving in the Union army, Harriet told an interviewer that at the

[13]Ibid., 104.
[14]Ibid.

time she was still upset with Lincoln. Yes, he had finally emancipated the slaves, but Harriet still didn't think it was right that the men who enlisted in Lincoln's army weren't given equal pay.

> I didn't like Lincoln in those days. I used to go see Mrs. Lincoln, but I never wanted to see him. You see, we colored people didn't understand that he was our friend. All we knew was that the first colored troops sent South from Massachusetts only got seven dollars a month, while the white got fifteen. We didn't like that.[15]

From the vantage point of the years, however, having put the president's life and works in perspective, Harriet concluded with some regret, "Now . . . I'm sorry I didn't go to see Mr. Lincoln."[16]

The Boston journey revived Harriet in every way, as most of her trips to that city had over the years, and Harriet was able to return to her work with the army. She went to a different post this time, however. The Sanitary Commission asked her to serve at Fortress Monroe, Virginia, where there was a freedman's hospital. Conditions there were deplorable, which greatly hindered the soldiers' recovery. There wasn't enough money for medical supplies, and manpower was at a severe shortage as well. Harriet worked as a nurse or "matron" and often went to Washington, D.C., to appeal to the government for more funds and supplies to improve the situation. She also would call on her old friend Secretary of State William Seward to see what he could do about getting equal pay for black soldiers. Unfortunately, there was only so much he could ac-

---

[15]Conrad, 187.
[16]Ibid.

complish against overwhelming odds—and prejudice.

On April 9, 1865, Harriet was at Fortress Monroe when the welcome news arrived that the war was over. That good and faithful servant had sacrificed three more years of her remarkable life to a cause much larger than herself, one for which she would have died gladly. Back home in Auburn she would be celebrated for her good works, but on the way to that beloved place, she came to understand how very much work remained ahead of her if blacks were ever going to be both free and equal.

As Harriet boarded the train for New York, a white conductor refused to honor her military pass, which entitled her to half the fare on the passenger cars. Upon seeing this black woman seated sedately along with white riders, he yelled, "Come, hustle out of here." When Harriet tried to explain the situation, producing all manner of credentials to support her argument, the man called her vile names. Then he disappeared briefly, but that wasn't the end of the affair. The conductor returned presently with three other men, who yanked Harriet from the passenger car, nearly wrenching off one arm in the process. They marched her through the train, past gaping passengers, then, with all their strength, pitched her into a baggage car. Suffering intensely from the attack, Harriet traveled home, where she remained in severe pain for months.[17]

On December 18 the Thirteenth Amendment to the U.S. Constitution was ratified, officially ending slavery in the United States and its territories. But what about prejudice? Had Harriet's mission to free her people really been fulfilled?

---

[17]Ibid., 188.

12

No Time to Rest

The strife was over, the battle done. The cause that Harriet and so many others had risked—and lost—their lives for was won; slavery in the United States was no more. There was no longer a need for an Underground Railroad, abolitionist rallies, and newspapers. Free blacks now could pursue their own lives on their own terms while once-proud slave owners sat on the ash heap of a costly and bitter defeat. Abraham Lincoln, who finally had made emancipation happen, had died at Ford's Theater shortly after Lee's surrender to Grant at Appomattox, Virginia. With the war behind it, America raced toward full industrialization and westward expansion.

The woman who had rescued some three hundred slaves before the war and who had given above and beyond any reasonable call of duty to the Union army, surely had earned the right to rest on her many laurels. For Harriet, it was time to forget the murky swamps and the bleeding feet, the hunger and loneliness, and the terrible risks she had endured to end slavery. The old way had passed.

Almost as a symbol of that former life was Harriet's first husband's death. According to an article that appeared in the October 7, 1867, *Baltimore American*, John Tubman and a white man, Robert Vincent, had a bitter argument one morning over what the paper described rather unintelligibly as "some ashes." Vincent became so enraged that he threatened Tubman's life and ended up chasing him away with an axe. Later that afternoon the two antagonists happened to meet on the road near Cambridge, Maryland. Tubman's thirteen-year-old son by his wife, Caroline, was with him at the time. Vincent asked if Tubman "was the same man as he was in the morning." Tubman replied that, yes, he was. Wordlessly, Vincent drove down the road some forty yards in his wagon and then, without warning, suddenly turned and shot Tubman several times, hitting him in the forehead, throat, and chest. With his son looking on in horror, Tubman died instantly on the road while Vincent drove on calmly, never bothering to see whether his opponent was dead or not. Although Vincent went to court on a murder charge, the jury found him not guilty.[1]

There would be many cases like this in the South as some embittered whites took out their anger over losing the war, and their former way of life, on those who no longer called them "master." Although John's distressing end saddened Harriet, she didn't lament over it any longer than she had his unfaithfulness to her. She had her family to enjoy and work yet to be done.

Some family members who had escaped from Maryland with Harriet's help lived close to her, and their presence and safety were a great source of joy for

---

[1]Conrad, 195.

her. She especially cherished having her parents live with her. Now in their nineties, Ben and Old Rit were familiar figures to the citizens of Auburn, who had helped to look after them in Harriet's absence.

In spite of their age and various ailments, the Rosses still went faithfully to church services every Sunday. First they walked a mile to the Central Church of Auburn, where they usually slept through the service. Afterward, they ventured to what was called a "class-meeting" at the Methodist Church in town, then stayed to attend a third worship service before slowly making their way back home. Harriet's beloved parents contributed much happiness to her life, as well as to the lives of everyone who knew those kind and honorable people.

Although Harriet could now live in peace, without fear of the lash or being sold to a chain gang, overcoming slavery had taken a physical toll on her. A few years after the war, when Harriet was about fifty years old, Sarah Bradford described her as "old and feeble, suffering from the effects of her life of unusual labor and hardship, as well as from repeated injuries."[2]

Harriet's worst ailment was the continued and prolonged bouts of somnolence that she endured from the effects of the lead weight attack way back in her youth. Harriet's friends talked to her about having surgery to relieve the pressure on her brain, and she decided to go ahead with it. She had the operation at Boston's Massachusetts General Hospital, but unfortunately the procedure didn't cure her or even give her relief. For the rest of her life, Harriet would live with that thorn in her flesh. She would suddenly fall asleep

---

[2]Bradford, 129.

up to three or four times a day, and people often came upon her in the middle of one of her "spells." One time a friend found her leaning against a fence during the day, as sound asleep as if it were nighttime and she were in her bed. The operation hadn't relieved her affliction, but Harriet had no intention of resting from her labors on behalf of blacks.

She believed that African-Americans needed her in freedom as badly as they ever had in bondage. Now that there was no longer any need for rescuing slaves from their masters, Harriet took on what she referred to as her "last work," which was to set up a hospital for aged and destitute blacks. She would name it after her dear friend and hero, John Brown.

In the pre-Civil War years, Harriet had used her Auburn home to comfort and house temporarily those runaways who were having trouble adjusting to life away from slavery. She had always provided shelter, clothing, food, and spiritual comfort for those who found their way to her. It was normal for her to have eight to ten people at one time under her roof. Now she needed to expand her base of operations to accommodate the growing needs of indigent blacks.

In addition to that project, Harriet also helped to raise funds for the creation of two freedman schools for young African-Americans in the South. She knew that literacy was going to help establish her people in their newly won freedom. Another thing that would help them was their spiritual maturation. As an active member of Auburn's A.M.E. Zion Church, Harriet helped to plant other A.M.E. congregations in the region to meet that need.

Harriet's new goals, which really were an extension of the earlier one to liberate her people so that they could live in God-given freedom, required money.

Unfortunately, Harriet had never known a time when her finances were steady or secure. The Lord, however, had always come through for her at just the right time to provide whatever she needed. During the years she had learned to depend on Him to supply all her needs according to His riches in glory. This time, one way that He helped was through the Freedman's Association of Boston. When the group discovered that Harriet was trying to establish a home for poor blacks, it decided to give her a ten-dollar monthly stipend. Ten dollars did not go very far, though. And when Harriet's mortgage came due in 1868, she found herself in a crisis. Unless she could meet that obligation, she was going to lose her home. Her parents and the others for whom she cared would be out on the streets.

Money became even tighter than usual. During the winter of 1867–68, severe rheumatism incapacitated Ben Ross. As a result, Harriet was now housebound, unable to earn any money because her father needed her almost-constant attention. One terrible day she realized that there was virtually no food left, so she put on her boots and trudged into town through heavy snowdrifts to her friend Annie's house. Harriet dreaded asking for help, but it was the only way she could figure out to deal with the near-desperate situation.

When Harriet reached her destination, she nervously started pacing up and down the room, which she usually did when she was deeply upset about something. Finally, she brought herself one step closer to the point of her visit.

"Miss Annie?"

"What, Harriet?" her friend asked kindly.

There was another lengthy pause, and then she repeated, "Miss Annie?"

"Well, what is it, Harriet?"

This exchange went on four times before Harriet found the courage to ask with tear-filled eyes and an aching heart, "Miss Annie, could you lend me a quarter till Monday? I never asked it before."

Miss Annie was happy to help out, and Harriet showed up on her doorstep with the quarter that Monday, just as she had promised.[3] The same woman who boldly could ask Thomas Garrett for twenty dollars to help slaves escape to the North found it difficult to request a fraction of that amount for her own use, although it really was to feed her family and her boarders.

Harriet sought other relief from the United States government when she applied for a military pension as an appropriate allowance for her faithful wartime service. She argued that the army owed her eighteen hundred dollars for her efforts on its behalf from 1862 to 1865. Unfortunately, the government avowed that because Harriet had never held a commission and because she didn't apply for compensation through "regular channels," it couldn't issue any benefits.[4] This upset Harriet and her friends, who believed that she was being cheated out of a legitimate pension. The drive to obtain payment for her began in earnest during the spring of 1868 with her friends Secretary of State William Seward, General David Hunter, surgeon Henry K. Durant, two congressmen, and some prominent citizens of Auburn eagerly taking up her excellent cause.

---

[3]Conrad, 202.
[4]Ibid.

Seeing her friend's acute financial distress and the disgraceful way in which the government Harriet had given to so unselfishly was treating her, Sarah Bradford decided to take her own action in the spring of 1868. Although she was not an experienced or published writer, Bradford interviewed Harriet extensively about her fascinating life with the goal of self-publishing the biography of the Moses of her people. Men like William Seward and Gerrit Smith helped finance publication of the book, which was called *Scenes in the Life of Harriet Tubman*.

The book came out in early 1869 and was a success. It netted twelve hundred dollars, which went directly to Harriet to pay off her mortgage on the house, as well as to assist in her home-based work with poor blacks. She was so thrilled about this financial boon that she often went about her work singing, "There's cider in the cellar, and the black folks, they'll have some; must be now the kingdom coming, and the year of Jubilum."[5]

Harriet's time of blessing did not last for very long, however. Within a few months of her fiscal windfall, Harriet once again found herself broke. She simply found it impossible to be prudent with money when she saw so many African-Americans in desperate need. After paying her mortgage, she sent some of what money was left to the southern freedman's schools that she supported. Then the remainder went to feeding and clothing "the brood that now hung upon her skirts."[6]

According to Harriet, the Lord had always come through in the past when she was in need, and she

[5]Ibid., 206.
[6]Ibid., 207.

trusted that His promises were for all time. She was to struggle financially for the rest of her life, but in no case would she turn anyone away who needed her, in spite of the burden that caring for so many people placed on her not only financially but physically and emotionally as well. This was the work the Lord had given her, and somehow He was going to take care of the material necessities of it.

Those who flocked to Harriet like wounded birds had many different kinds of needs. Some were lame and blind. There were also abandoned and abused children, as well as those who suffered from mental instability. All were candidates for her vast reserves of compassion.

The people of Auburn loved and respected Harriet for her works of mercy, and responded by providing food and money to help whenever they could. Although most people would have been exhausted just by feeding, nursing, and cleaning up after so many people, Harriet thrived on her labors because she loved caring for people so much. As a beneficial side effect, when she was working hard she didn't succumb so readily to her sleeping spells.

In addition to her household duties, Harriet also grew produce on her land. What wasn't consumed would be peddled from door to door so that she could earn as much of her livelihood as possible, without depending on others. Her customers often would invite her to come inside for a snack in hopes that Harriet might sit awhile and regale them with one of her gripping stories of life on the Underground Railroad or in the Civil War.

One woman who often asked Harriet to stay for a bit revealed a touching point about Harriet's uncomplicated and unaffected character. The incident shows how little Harriet asked of life for herself, while giving so much to others. The woman commented first on her physical appearance: "Harriet, when I knew her in her matriarchal phase, was a magnificent-looking woman, [a] true African, with a broad nose [and] very black. [She was] of medium height." Then she spoke of the simple pleasure Harriet got out of one very small gesture of hospitality, one little reward for all of her sacrificial service to others. "I used to often sit and listen to her stories when I could get her to tell them. We always gave her something to eat. She preferred butter in her tea to anything else. That was a luxury. . . ."[7]

[7]Ibid., 211.

13

The Struggle Continues

In the postwar years, Harriet continued to labor in the vineyard of the Lord, and she flourished with the good works she did in His strength. In fact, it has been said that the African-American community in Auburn, New York, revolved around Harriet.[1] Whenever she gave her testimony at church, for example, they flocked to hear her, and brought others to listen.

Harriet's life was mostly striving and building for her people, but something else entirely contributed to her personal happiness during this time. On March 18, 1869, she took a husband.

Nelson Davis was a veteran of Company G, Eighth U.S. Colored Infantry Volunteers. He served the Union army from September 1863 to November 1865, and had seen action in Florida at the battle of Olustee, as well as other campaigns. He also contracted tuberculosis as a soldier. Davis met Harriet while in South Carolina, perhaps while he was in the hospital. It isn't clear when or how they got to know each other or what

---

[1]Conrad, 212.

drew them together. Did they pursue a relationship at that time, or after the war? Whatever the answers may have been, Nelson was a man of excellent judgment. "He had the respect of his fellowmen, and he knew that Harriet Tubman was a rare and an unusual woman."[2]

Davis, himself born into slavery, remains an obscure figure. Among the few facts known about him was his age: he was more than twenty years younger than Harriet, very unusual for married couples in the Victorian era. Some scholars have speculated that Harriet simply wanted to take care of Davis because he was sick and in need. If that had been the case, however, why wouldn't she have simply invited him to live in her home along with other blacks for whom she cared? Was it considered scandalous that she married someone young enough to be her son? It is possible that this is one reason why so little has been written about Davis.

Nevertheless, their wedding was a rousing social event in Auburn, and U.S. Secretary Seward joined other "first families of the city" at the racially diverse evening ceremony in Central Church. The Reverend Henry Fowler presided over the unusual affair. An unidentified Auburn newspaper gave the following account:

> Before a large and very select audience, Harriet Tubman . . . took unto herself a husband and made one William Nelson (Nelson Davis) a happy man. Both born slaves, as they grew in years and knowledge recognized the glory of freedom, still later in the eventful struggle they fled from bondage, until finally, by the blessing of Divine Provi-

---

[2]Ibid., 206.

dence, they stood there, last evening, free, and were joined as man and wife. . . . After the ceremony, Rev. Mr. Fowler made some very touching and happy allusions to their past trials, and the apparently plain sailing the parties now had. . . . The ceremony ended amid the congratulations of the assembly, and the happy couple were duly embarked on the journey of life.[3]

According to Harriet's great-niece, Mariline Wilkins, Davis was an easygoing man who didn't care to bring attention to himself. He helped Harriet in her work by farming her small parcel of land. He was, on the whole, entirely devoted to her and her mission.

Indeed, her work did not abate in the years following the wedding. She went on helping to spread A.M.E. churches throughout central and western New York, and she gave interviews to various Christian journals, including the Salvation Army's magazine, *The Evangelist*, which helped secure funds for her ministry. Along with her friends from abolitionist days, Susan B. Anthony (who helped outfit Harriet's slaves on their way to Canada several times) and Elizabeth Cady Stanton, Harriet also continued to speak out for women's suffrage—an effort that was likely supported by her husband—attending local meetings whenever possible.

Once she went to a Rochester church for a women's event in which both Anthony and Stanton were on the platform. They had noticed her come in. Finding it warm in the church, Harriet promptly went to sleep. She was a much-loved and venerable figure by then, and her presence at such a meeting was something to draw attention to. Anthony said to the assembly,

---

[3]Ibid., 214.

"Friends, we have in the audience that wonderful woman Harriet Tubman, from whom we should like to hear, if she will kindly come to the platform." It took the people around the sleeping woman no little time to rouse her and tell her that she had been summoned to go forward and make some remarks. One lady walked with her to the podium, and a glowing Susan B. Anthony introduced her. "Ladies," she said, "I am glad to present to you Harriet Tubman, the conductor of the Underground Railroad."

"Yes, ladies, I was the conductor of the Underground Railroad," Harriet told the assembly, "and I can say what most conductors can't say—I never ran my train off the track and I never lost a passenger." Now fully awake, she went on to tell them some exciting stories from her past and why their cause was just as noble.[4] Harriet, along with other female abolitionists including Harriet Beecher Stowe, Lucretia Mott, and Sojourner Truth, had helped guide the nation out of the swamp of slavery. Shouldn't they now, went one of the arguments for suffrage, be permitted to cast their ballots, to be used by God to mend the country's other flaws?

Despite Harriet's being a cherished and highly respected figure in the postwar years, there were people who sought to take advantage of her "unfailing faith in the essential goodness of human nature."[5] And although she usually exercised excellent judgment about people, at times she faltered. A case in point was a scandal that made the national news in 1873.

Two southern blacks claimed to have five thousand dollars in gold that one of them, a fellow named Har-

[4]Ibid., 207.
[5]Ibid., 210.

ris, said he had simply stumbled upon during the war. They hadn't exchanged it for greenbacks in the South, however, because they feared—rightly—that the government would confiscate the gold. Instead, they went up north with it, finding themselves in Seneca Falls, New York, where they looked for vulnerable people to swindle. One of them was Harriet's brother John Stewart.

He was sufficiently impressed with their "get-rich-quick" scheme to tell Harriet how she could stand to make a good deal of money by purchasing their gold cheaply. Here was a great opportunity to make some money for Harriet's home for poor blacks. She was broke, and yet she so passionately wanted to establish a hospital for blacks and name it after her cherished John Brown that she foolishly entered into a risky venture in order to make it happen.

Although Harriet listened to the men and became convinced that they had a valuable service to offer, some of her close friends became immediately suspicious of their motives and cautioned her not to have anything to do with them. It is likely that if William Seward, who had often advised her, had still been alive, he probably would have recognized the makings of a scam and talked her out of it. But he had died the year before. Instead, another friend, Anthony Shimer, eagerly came forward with two thousand dollars that he was willing to exchange on Harriet's behalf for the gold.

Harriet, her husband, brother, and three friends, including Shimer, went to meet the con men in a forest in the county's south end. Somehow, Harriet and the money became separated from her friends, and the tricksters attacked and robbed her. After she was bound and gagged, she passed out. It was one of the few incidents in her glorious life "in which she emerged as the loser."[6]

For the most part, Harriet had excellent instincts and sound judgment, combined with caution and prayerful vigilance whenever she acted on something of importance. She was enormously successful in life as a result. It is, however, an indication of her humanity that she was not without occasional lapses of judgment. For example, sharing Harriet's family life in Auburn was her niece, a young woman with whom she was especially close. Margaret Stewart was the daughter of one of Harriet's brothers, probably John, who, like many free blacks, had taken his employer's last name. Although Harriet was profoundly devoted to the girl, and vice versa, the relationship had an ignominious beginning, according to Margaret's mother.

When he was researching the life of Harriet Tubman in the late 1930s, Earl Conrad received a revealing letter from Miss Stewart's daughter, Mrs. A. J. Brickler of Ohio. Mrs. Brickler said that Margaret, her twin brother, and their other siblings, all had been born free. Margaret's father had apparently purchased his freedom from the John Stewart who had run the timber business in which Harriet, her father, and several brothers had worked. Her mother had never been a slave.

In Mrs. Brickler's letter, she made the extraordinary statement that her mother, Margaret Stewart, was "kidnapped" by Aunt Harriet. Although Margaret Stewart's early memories of the South were vague, amounting to her recollection of some family possessions, including "a pair of slick chestnut horses and a shiny carriage," the one outstanding recollection was

---

[6]Ibid., 74.

of her Aunt Harriet's visit.[7] No doubt, any black child would be excited by the clandestine visit of the famous slave rescuer, Moses—more so if it happened to be her aunt. Mrs. Brickler said that when Harriet first saw Margaret she "fell in love with the little girl who was my mother," then she speculated as to why that had been the case.

> Maybe it was because in mother she saw the child she herself might have been if slavery had been less cruel. Maybe it was because she knew the joys of motherhood would never be hers and she longed for some little creature who would love her for her own self's sake.[8]

Part of the attraction also might have been that Margaret bore a striking resemblance to Harriet. In this matter, however, as in few others, Harriet used poor judgment, according to Mrs. Brickler. She relied instead on her overwhelming affection for the child.

When it was time for Harriet to say good-bye to her emancipated brother and his family, she secretly snatched Margaret and went away with her. Brickler speculated, "I wonder what her thoughts could have been as she and her little partner stood side by side on the deck of the steamer looking far out over the water."[9]

Actually, Harriet almost immediately had misgivings, feeling a keen sense of remorse for what she had done. She had taken her brother's daughter from a secure home without his or his wife's knowledge or consent. What would Harriet do with the child once she

---

[7]Ibid.
[8]Ibid., 74–75.
[9]Ibid., 75.

reached the North, especially living a lifestyle that was so unpredictable, unsettled, and precarious? "She knew she had violated her brother's home and sorrow and anger were there," Brickler wrote.[10]

Harriet ended up leaving Margaret in Mrs. William Seward's care. It proved to be a good move in the long run. The white woman brought Margaret up, not as a servant, but as a "guest within her home," giving her many educational, spiritual, and social advantages.[11] Mrs. Brickler said, "This kindly lady . . . taught mother to speak properly, to read, write, sew, do housework and act as a lady."[12]

In telling this story, Earl Conrad took pains to emphasize the lifelong devotion that existed between Margaret and Harriet, and when he told Mrs. Brickler's story, he put the word *kidnapped* in quotations, as if to soften the effect of what was certainly explosive material. He also tried to explain the strong ties that bound Harriet and her niece:

> There is only one explanation for the unbroken, life-long shower of affection which Harriet vented upon this girl. It grew out of Harriet's dislocated life. She was warm enough to require and to have the most personal emotions, to have a need for a husband, and a need for her own children; and her affection for Margaret Stewart, in some way, supplied this lack.[13]

It apparently isn't known how Harriet's brother or his wife responded to the situation when they realized what had happened. That they made no known at-

[10]Ibid.
[11]Ibid.
[12]Ibid.
[13]Ibid., 74.

tempt to bring their child home would seem to indicate their acceptance of the circumstances. Indeed, if Margaret's father was John Stewart, he ended up settling around Auburn himself, most likely with his wife and other children. Margaret's intense affection for her aunt reveals her own lack of animosity toward the woman. Both her and her parents' reactions provide an extraordinary tribute to Harriet Tubman's overall character.

With Margaret nearby, Harriet's husband and her parents to care for (Ben and Old Rit both lived until they were nearly 100), as well as a house full of people and a rich relationship with God, Harriet had a full and satisfying life. She often received visitors who made their way to the Adirondacks first to see John Brown's grave and then to Auburn to see her. Among them was the vibrant young black scholar Booker T. Washington, who became a frequent guest in her home. In the final decades of the nineteenth century, however, Harriet stood by and watched as her friends from abolitionist days passed away. In fact, she would go on to outlive most of them. Sadly, Harriet also outlived her husband, who died on October 14, 1888, most likely of tuberculosis. He was only forty-four at his death, and she was sixty-eight.

Two years later, on June 27, 1890, Congress passed a pension act that enabled widows of Civil War veterans to receive benefits. Harriet applied for and received an eight-dollar monthly payment. Her repeated requests for compensation in her own name for the work she had done during the war were never honored.

Throughout the 1890s people sent letters to national newspapers and various congressmen proclaiming that a woman with a war record such as Harriet's should be honored with her own recompense. When a bill came before Congress in 1899, and the debate about her service was entered in the *Congressional Record*, the story further secured for her a place in the pages of American history. Congressmen from New York, in particular, took up her cause, requesting a twenty-five dollar per month pension to cover both Harriet and her husband's war services. Finally, in 1902, she was awarded twenty dollars per month for the rest of her life, but only as Mrs. Nelson Davis, Civil War widow, and not for her own efforts in the war.[14]

[14]Another woman, a white lady named Anna Ella Carroll, had served on the Tennessee River during the war and also was ultimately denied a pension in spite of petitioning the government, like Harriet, for years.

14

Eternal Freedom

Harriet was called Moses because she delivered her people from bondage, but she also had much in common with the apostle Paul. The perils he faced in carrying out God's will read like adventures from Harriet's own life.

> I have been constantly on the move. I have been in danger from rivers, in danger from bandits, in danger from my own countrymen . . . in danger in the city, in danger in the country, in danger at sea; and in danger from false brothers. I have labored and toiled and have often gone without sleep; I have known hunger and thirst and have often gone without food; I have been cold and naked. Besides everything else, I face daily the pressure of my concern for all the churches. (2 Cor. 11:26–28)

Like Paul, Harriet also had learned the "secret" of contentment in spite of all the dangers, toils, and snares; she did all things through Christ, who strengthened her (Phil. 4:13).

Harriet bore the lingering effects of her most ominous days of rescue and escape, spying and nursing, long after those days had passed. Writing in the 1886 second edition of her biography about Harriet, Sarah Bradford noted, "That poor neck is even now covered with the scars which sixty years of life have not been able to efface."[1] This literal statement may be taken symbolically as well; Harriet endured many other scars from those brave times. And like those distant days, she remained as determined as ever to continue caring for the needs of African-Americans now that they were free. Having rescued so many of her people from "the land of Egypt," Harriet "sought to make meaningful the promise of freedom."[2]

Harriet's "last work" from the Lord, to create a proper hospital for Auburn's poor blacks, had yet to be accomplished. In the meantime she was exhausting the limits of her own home, where she had been taking care of them since the end of the war. Now Harriet asked God to let her live until the hospital was established. She wanted her closing efforts to be devoted to caring for "those for whom she had already risked so much."[3] Then she would be ready to go. Many of the leading townspeople supported Harriet's noble goal, including the mayor and his wife, who helped her organize meetings to drum up support for the facility. It took years, however, for the vision she planted to bear fruit.

When Harriet was well into her seventies, "aged far beyond her years" and suffering from prolonged and frequent bouts of somnolence, she made a bold move. She bid $1,450 at a June 1896 auction to ac-

---

[1]Bradford, 21.
[2]Ibid., x.
[3]Ibid., 7.

quire the twenty-five acres next to her home.[4] At the time, she had no money to speak of, but that had never stopped Harriet from acting before. She described what the auction was like:

> They were all white folks but me, there, and there I was like a blackberry in a pail of milk, but I hid down in a corner, and no one knew who was bidding. The man began down pretty low, and I kept going up by fifties. At last I got up to fourteen hundred and fifty, and the other stopped bidding, and the man said, "All done. Who is the buyer?" "Harriet Tubman," I shouted.[5]

Harriet went down to a bank and borrowed the money for her new property. She wanted to call her facility the John Brown Home, as she had been dreaming about all along, but she didn't have enough funds to incorporate it. A few years later, in 1903, Harriet deeded both the twenty-five acres and her own home to the A.M.E. Zion Church of Auburn. Five years later her wish was fulfilled when the new center officially opened as the John Brown Home. It could accommodate between ten and twelve people and was open to African-Americans of all ages and conditions, both sick and strong, whoever was in any type of need. A woman named Frances Smith, a dear friend of Harriet's, served as its matron. By then Harriet was over eighty years old.

The venture did not go smoothly. Harriet became upset that after she deeded the property to the church, the home began to require a one-hundred-dollar entrance fee. She had never asked for anything from

---

[4]Ibid., x.
[5]Conrad, 220.

those who came to her in distress. She didn't believe it was right to take care of the destitute and sick by requiring them to turn over money they didn't have. The home's administrators, on the other hand, believed that while her intentions certainly were honorable, it wasn't practical to run a free institution.

Harriet also made her position known that the John Brown Home should have an interracial board of directors. From the time she had entered the world of the Underground Railroad, on to her work with the Union army, she had learned the importance of cooperation between whites and blacks in advancing her people's cause. Other board members wanted to depend only on the black community, though, to support the home. Harriet knew that wouldn't work because blacks did not possess sufficient financial resources. When a special vote was taken to settle the matter, she found herself outnumbered; the board was to consist only of black members. Sadly, her convictions eventually were proven correct—the John Brown Home closed just a few years after her death due to lack of funding.[6]

Harriet's life wasn't *all* bureaucratic red tape and political argument. Well into her advanced age, she enjoyed life, especially her ability to travel freely around New York and Massachusetts without fear of being caught and sent back into slavery. One of her quirks was that she never bothered much with train

---

[6]Another facility for poor black women, established in 1904 in Boston as the Harriet Tubman Home, had both whites and blacks at the helm, and it continued to operate at least until the 1940s. Harriet had given her blessing to its founder, Julia O. Henderson, to establish a place for Boston's needy black women and to name it after her. Harriet even attended the dedication ceremony. It was among the first homes of its kind to be named after Harriet during her life. Several more were created after her death.

schedules. If she had some place to go, she simply went to the station and waited patiently for the first train to come along.

As a celebrity, Harriet was recognized wherever she went. She was especially noticed and venerated in Auburn, where people would point and whisper, "There goes Harriet Tubman!" In 1902, when she attended a gathering for suffragists at the home of Eliza Wright Osborne, Susan B. Anthony, who was also there, wrote an enthusiastic account of the meeting to a friend:

> This most wonderful woman—Harriet Tubman—is still alive. . . . All of us were visiting at the Osbornes', a real love feast of the few [abolitionists] that are left and here came Harriet Tubman![7]

Because Harriet was so greatly venerated, she was often invited to attend special events. Her presence was even coveted by the Queen of England. In 1897, at the time of her sixtieth anniversary on the throne, Queen Victoria sent a Diamond Jubilee medal to Harriet and extended an invitation to her to come to Great Britain as her special guest. Although Harriet declined, not wishing to travel that far, she greatly cherished the queen's letter and once told someone that it "was worn to a shadow, so many people read it."[8]

Although the years had exacted a great deal from her physically, Harriet took pains to look her best, priding herself on maintaining a pleasant, yet simple, appearance. There is a description of her during these later years, provided by Mrs. Emily Hopkins Drake,

[7]Conrad, 214.
[8]Ibid., 215.

who had some photos taken of the great woman. She recalled that although Harriet had become "shriveled" in her appearance, she still made an effort to look attractive:

> I remember the day we took those snaps, how Harriet went to a mirror, and tied on her cape, pulling out the ribbons that held it, and the white ruffle about her throat with as much care and pride as a young girl. Her dress was a neat percale as I remember it, dull in color. I should say, a gray and white stripe, though I am not positive about that. The hat was a battered old black straw with ribbon trimming.[9]

As she had in her younger years, Harriet still expressed great joy in singing, something that also blessed those around her. Mrs. Drake recalled, "We always loved to hear her sing, and I remember vividly how she would rock to and fro, pounding her hands on her knees in time to the rhythm."[10]

Reporters often showed up at Harriet's home, asking her to tell them about her more youthful and adventurous days. Although she was frequently bound to a wheelchair in her last years and suffered acutely from rheumatism and sleeping spells, she was obliging. She delighted to tell stories about how faithful God had been to her in every circumstance as she led her people out of bondage.

In 1907 a reporter for the *New York Herald* sat with her outside her home as she regaled him with anecdotes of her days as Moses. During the end of the interview, Harriet pointed toward an orchard in the

---

[9]Ibid., 222.
[10]Ibid.

near distance and asked him, "Do you like apples?" The man said that he did. "Did you ever plant any apple trees?" He hadn't. "No, but somebody else planted them," she said. "I liked apples when I was young, and I said, 'Someday I'll plant apples myself for the other young folks to eat,' and I guess I did it."[11]

In 1911 James B. Clarke, who was writing a pamphlet about Harriet to raise funds for the John Brown Home, also interviewed her. He was impressed that although she was then over ninety, she had gone downstairs on the morning of their first discussion without assistance and that later she had eaten such an enormous dinner that it would "tax the stomach of a gourmand."[12] At one point Harriet became upset when her nurse suggested that she be fed when all she wanted was to have her chicken cut up and a tray placed in her lap.

In another interview conducted that same year, the Geneva, New York, suffrage leader, Elizabeth Smith Miller, came to call. Miller asked her a pointed question: "Do you really believe that women should vote?" Harriet seemed surprised by it and responded, "I suffered enough to believe it."[13]

Harriet may have been old, but she never lost her youthful zeal for life or her sense of fun as age wore her body down. One day she played a prank on her eight- or nine-year-old great-grandniece, Alice Lucas, who was playing in the yard. The child became frightened at the sight of something slithering in the grass behind her, only to discover that it was her Aunt Harriet, crawling around as if she were still in her Underground Railroad or Civil War days.

---

[11]Ibid., 191.
[12]Ibid., 222.
[13]Ibid., 217.

During a particularly difficult illness, Harriet was taken to the Auburn City Hospital. Afterward she was discharged to the home that she had founded to meet the needs of others, where she spent the rest of her life. In the Sunday, June 25, 1911, issue of the *New York World* under the headline "Moses of Her Race Ending Her Life in Home She Founded," it was reported:

> She was the friend of great men, but now, almost a centenarian, she awaits the last call. Now, with the weight of almost a hundred years on her shoulders, she seeks rest during the few remaining days.[14]

The last time Harriet made it to church, heaven was very much on her mind. She told a hushed congregation,

> I am nearing the end of my journey; I can hear them bells a-ringing, I can hear the angels singing, I can see the hosts a-marching, I hear someone say, "There is one crown left and that is for Old Aunt Harriet and she shall not lose her reward."[15]

On November 18, 1912, Harriet made out her will. In it she left her worldly goods in equal portions to her niece Mary Gaston, and her grandniece Katy Stewart, a daughter of Margaret Stewart, as well as to her unfailing companion and matron of the home, Frances Smith. Then, her worldly and spiritual affairs in order, bedridden and with only weeks left to live, Harriet received her final visitors. Among them was the distinguished black suffragette Mary B. Talbert, who

---

[14]Ibid., 223.
[15]Ibid.

directed the New York State Federation of Colored Women's Clubs. Harriet told Mrs. Talbert how happy she was in the John Brown Home, commenting on the "sweet spirit" that she sensed all around the place. When Mrs. Talbert rose to leave, Harriet took her hand firmly and urged her to tell the women in the cause of suffrage to "stand together."[16]

In her final weeks, Harriet suffered greatly from pneumonia. Nevertheless, she remained fully aware of everything and everyone around her until just a few hours before she died. As her beloved friends and relatives gathered around her bed to pray for her, she actually participated in the prayers. She expressed her dedication to the good of her people and to the God she had loved and followed her entire life.

So many people came to see Harriet that the home finally had to limit the number of her visitors, much to her disappointment. On March 10 she asked for a few of her friends to stay with her. She also expressed regret that she couldn't receive Eliza E. Peterson, the superintendent for temperance work among blacks, who had come all the way from Texas to see her. Harriet sent word, however, to the woman that she should greet those in black temperance work for her.

With just hours left in her long, earthly journey, two ministers came to her and held a service in which she participated. People waiting outside the room reported hearing her voice singing "Swing Low, Sweet Chariot." That evening, March 10, 1913, the chariot arrived to carry her home. She was ninety-three. The next day's *Auburn Citizen* reported that "the final scene in the long drama of her life was quite as thrill-

---

[16]Ibid., 224.

ing as the many that had gone before."[17]

Auburn, New York, did not forget its favorite daughter. A little over a year later, on Friday, June 12, 1914, the city where Harriet had spent so much of her life staged a moving tribute to her. That Thursday, Mayor Charles W. Brister issued a proclamation that appeared under the following newspaper headline: "Let All Display Flags on the Morrow! Is the Official Wish of Mayor Brister, That the Memory of Faithful Old Slave Harriet Tubman May Be Honored." The declaration read,

> The citizens of Auburn have very properly seen fit to erect a public monument to the memory of Harriet Tubman, as a tribute for her faithful services to the Nation, during the Civil War, and to her own people in the cause of freedom. As a further mark of respect and as a token of appreciation for her loyal and patriotic service to our country and flag, as Auburn's Chief Executive Officer, I direct that on tomorrow, June 12, the date of the unveiling of the memorial, the flags be displayed on the municipal buildings, and suggest as there are many of our loyal citizens who may wish to honor the memory of this faithful old slave who was willing to die for her race, if need be, that they also at the same time cooperate and display the national emblem from their homes and places of business.
>
> If the stars and stripes could float from every home in Auburn we believe that it would inspire patriotism and demonstrate that we are not forgetful of those who suffered for the cause of freedom and were willing to die that we might have one country and one flag.[18]

---

[17]Ibid.
[18]Ibid., 225.

The following day, the flags of a largely white city waved in the brilliant June sun as a tribute to the black Moses, something "unprecedented" in American history.[19] At Auburn's auditorium those flags were lowered to half-mast out of respect for Harriet when a bronze tablet in her honor was unveiled. The townspeople had paid for it through voluntary donations.

Many leading citizens of the Auburn, as well as the larger African-American, community were there, including Harriet's old friend Booker T. Washington. At a speech that night, he said that among her accomplishments, she had "brought the two races nearer together, made it possible for the white race to place a higher estimate upon the black race."[20] Afterward, the mayor told the audience that Harriet wasn't being honored primarily because of her color or her sex, but because of her great character, a theme that Martin Luther King Jr. would repeat some fifty years later at the March on Washington.

America has never forgotten this woman of most humble origins, a woman who loved others so much that she was willing to lay down her life for them, a faithful woman who depended on God in all things and who believed that when He made a promise, He meant what He said.

---

[19]Ibid.
[20]Ibid.

Bibliography

Blockson, Charles L. *The Underground Railroad*. New York: Prentice Hall Press, 1987.

Blockson, Charles L. *The Underground Railroad in Pennsylvania*. Jacksonville, N.C.: Flame International, 1981.

Bontemps, Arna. *Free at Last: The Life of Frederick Douglass*. New York: Dodd, Mead & Company, 1971.

Bradford, Sarah. *Harriet Tubman: The Moses of Her People*. Secaucus, N.J.: The Citadel Press, 1961.

Buckmaster, Henrietta. *Flight to Freedom*. New York: Thomas Y. Crowell, 1958.

Conrad, Earl. *Harriet Tubman*. Washington, D.C.: The Associated Publishers, 1943.

Cornish, Dudley Taylor. *The Sable Army: Black Troops in the Union Army, 1861–1865*. Lawrence, Ks.: University Press of Kansas, 1987.

Genovese, Eugene, et al. *The World the Slaves Made*. New York: Vintage Books, 1972.

Hamilton, Virginia. *Many Thousand Gone*. New York: Alfred A. Knopf, 1993.

Haskins, Jim. *Get on Board*. New York: Scholastic, Inc., 1993.

Hogrogian, Robert. *Harriet Tubman*. Hawthorne,

N.J.: January Productions, 1979.

Janney, Rebecca Price. *Great Women in American History*. Camp Hill, Pa.: Horizon Books, 1996.

Metzger, Milton, ed. *Frederick Douglass: In His Own Words*. San Diego: Harcourt Brace and Co., 1995.

Morison, Samuel Eliot. *The Oxford History of the American People*. New York: Oxford University Press, 1965.

Nies, Judith. *Seven Women: Portraits From the American Radical Tradition*. New York: Viking Press, 1977.

Sterling, Philip, and Rayford Logan. *Four Took Freedom: The Lives of Harriet Tubman, Frederick Douglass, Robert Smalls, and Blanche K. Bruce*. Garden City, N.Y.: Zenith Books, 1967.

Still, William. *Underground Railroad Records*. Philadelphia: William Still, Publisher, 1883.

Underground Railroad. Washington, D.C.: Division of Publications, National Park Service, 1998.

Dedication and Acknowledgments

I am especially grateful to the following people for helping me gain a better understanding of Harriet Tubman and of the Underground Railroad in general:

The tour guides at Mother Bethel A.M.E. Church in Philadelphia, and Mrs. Dockens, its founder Richard Allen's descendant, for introducing me to Harriet Tubman's great-niece, Mariline Wilkins.

Mrs. Wilkins, who gave me details about Harriet's life that I couldn't find in other places, as well as a family member's viewpoint; Harriet raised Mrs. Wilkins's mother from the age of nine.

Jackie Wiggins of the Johnson House Historic Site, Germantown, Pennsylvania, who provided fascinating insights about the brave Quaker family who hid runaways in their home. Joanna Hause, the librarian at Biblical Theological Seminary, who found a microfilm of William Still's 1883 book, as well as other hard-to-find volumes about Harriet's life, and her associate, Ruth Meyer, who did much legwork on my behalf. God bless you both for not running in the other direction when you saw me coming!

My precious husband, Scott, proofreader par excellence, who challenges me to do my very best, and who also endures my alternate bursts of enthusiasm and spaciness when I'm writing.

Finally, I dedicate this book to all who willingly lay down their lives for others, especially my sisters in Christ, Marlene Ciranowicz and the "One Heart" fellowship.

Other books by Rebecca Price Janney:

Great Letters in American History
Great Stories in American History
Great Women in American History

THE IMPOSSIBLE DREAMERS SERIES:

> *Secret of the Lost Colony*
> *The Mystery of Loch Ness*
> *Search for Amelia Earhart*

THE HEATHER REED MYSTERY SERIES:

> *The Cryptic Clue*
> *The Model Mystery*
> *The Eerie Echo*
> *The Toxic Secret*
> *The Major League Mystery*
> *The Exchange Student's Secret*
> *The Trail of Fear*
> *The Reins of Danger*